DON'T CALL ME ROVER!!

5001
NAMES TO CALL YOUR PET

RITA BLOCKTON

AVON BOOKS ◆ NEW YORK

AVON BOOKS
A division of
The Hearst Corporation
1350 Avenue of the Americas
New York, New York 10019

First Avon Books Trade Printing: March 1997

AVON TRADEMARK REG. U.S. PAT. OFF. AND IN OTHER COUNTRIES, MARCA REGISTRADA, HECHO EN U.S.A.

Printed in the U.S.A.

OPM   10   9   8   7   6   5   4   3   2   1

To Jesse and Adam . . . my two wonderful sons,
whose support, wit, and understanding have been
immeasurably gratifying.

Acknowledgments

I would like to thank Joan Caplin for her marvelous attention to detail, impressive mind, and much appreciated help; Mikey Stern for helping with all those sports names and nicknames; my friends for not running away from me when they saw that I was still working on "that name book"; and Lou Aronica for saving a very nearly lost cause.

And, finally, to all my past, present (and future) pets . . .

Chico
  Tusha
    Daisy I
      Daisy II
        and . . . Homer

Contents

Introduction

CONGRATULATIONS!!
Presumably you're about to buy, or have just gotten, a dog, cat, gerbil, cockatoo . . . just had a litter of something . . . or, maybe you're taking over a farm and have hundreds of wonderful cows or horses to name! Whatever it might be, if you're anything like me, half the fun of getting a new animal is naming it.

At first I tried to stay away from the usual . . . Tuffy, Taffy, Ginger (you wouldn't believe how many Gingers there are) . . . Rover & Fido (you wouldn't believe how FEW Rovers and Fidos there are). Well, in the end, I included them all. Hours in the library, at the vet's, looking through baby name books, magazines, television shows, dictionaries, thesauruses, almanacs, calling my friends . . . generally obsessing, as I tend to do.

Of course, I must admit that I made up a lot of them myself. Naming things is something I love to do. It all started in high school when I made up the name for our winter dance.

I actually won the naming contest! THE SNOW BALL (what can I tell you). So, while not exactly brilliant, I won two tickets to the dance, and, if you can imagine, THAT started me on a lifetime of naming things. (Now why couldn't I have won something everyone would have remembered me for, like a BEAUTY contest?! No one ever forgets who wins a beauty contest. I can assure you that no one even remembers that fateful dance, no less the name! No less WHO named it!)

But, since this seems to be my "thing," I hope you can sit back and enjoy looking through this book . . . and, with any luck, find the PURRFECT name for your pet!

Rita Blockton

How to Use This Book

When I got my pets, there were no pet naming books. I found that I spent hours, even days, trying to think up the perfect name. Realizing that many of us go through an intricate process when naming a pet, I decided that, not only would it have helped me to have a book to refer to, but, it could also have been fun at the same time. And that's how the concept for *Don't Call Me Rover!!* was born.

The real idea is to supply you with as many names as possible— the descriptions are there just for fun . . . so, while you may agree that 'Sylvester' should be for a cat, you may just as strongly, feel that it should be for a dog or bird . . . Go for it!

Have fun.

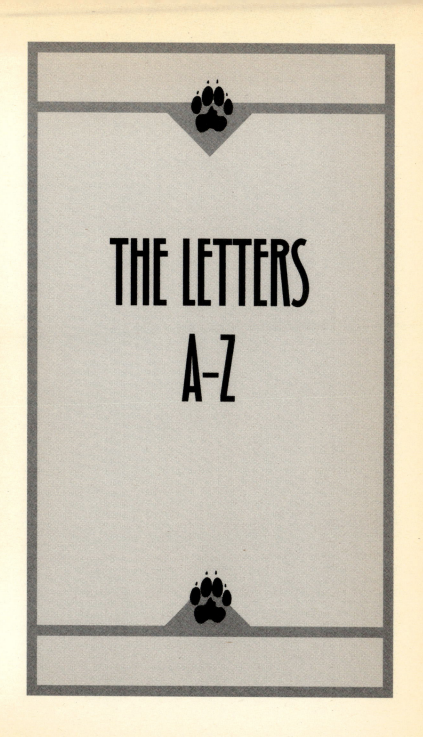

THE LETTERS
A-Z

A & D	Your pet helps with the baby diapers
A & E	For an arts & entertainment type
A & P	It loves to go food shopping
A & R	A pet for someone in the record industry
A LA CARTE	A waiter's pet
A LA MODE	An ice cream fanatic's pet
A.M.	An early morning pet
ABACUS	A mathematician's pet
ABBEY CAT	Perfect for an Abyssinian
ABBOTT	For someone whose first name is Bud or whose last name is Costello
ABC	See "Triples," with NBC and CBS
ABDUL-JABBAR	You love basketball
ABDULLAH	Pharaoh hounds or sloughis . . . originally from Egypt
ABE	My father's name . . . nice, kind, and a good cook
ABERCROMBIE	The great clothing store ABERCROMBIE & FITCH . . . 57th Street in Manhattan. Malls here and there

ABIGAIL	You have a Blue-cream point Himalayan, very female
ABIGAYLE	(Heb) Father is rejoicing. You notice that's not my name
ABLE	Pair with Cain
ABNER	'Lil Abner . . . the cartoon series.
ABOU	Means 'father' in Arabic. So, probably a good name for a stud animal
ABOUT TIME	You waited a long time to get it
ABRACADABRA	A wonderful name for a pet who keeps disappearing
ABRAHAM	The long version of my father's name, Abe. Still nice, kind, and a good cook
ABSOLUT	Swedish elkhound
ABSTRACT	Your pet has strange markings
ACE	The Ace of Hearts. Although, it seems like a real GUY name
ACHILLES	Heel!
ACTOR	For any animal who knows how to get the better of you
AD LIB	For any animal that can talk you into something
ADAM	It's your first. Pair with Eve and stay away from snakes
ADDYNUFF	You're always yelling at it
ADEL	My mother's friend while growing up in Larchmont
ADELSON	Good for a Pyrenees mastiff . . . powerful, big, silent, friendly, and not too interested in food (what a concept)
ADIEU	You travel a lot
ADMIRAL	Bulldogs, boxers, pugs
ADOLFO	It would have to be a very well dressed pet
ADOLPH	A good meat tenderizer . . . A German shepherd or Doberman pinscher

ADONIS	A great-looking male. No one I know. No one I'll ever meet. Your best of breed
ADORABELLE	Cats, Mini's
ADRIENNE	YO!!
AEROSMITH	Your pet has aspirations to be in a rock band
AEROSTAR	Great for any type of bird
AFRICA	As in *Out Of* . . .
AFRICAN QUEEN	Perfect for a black Turkish Angora . . . lush coat and regal looking
AFRICAN VIOLET	A white Turkish Angora . . . lush coat, not as regal looking as the queen
AGAMEMNON	Mythical Greek king of Mycenae during Trojan War . . . killed by his wife, Clytemnestra. Could spell trouble
AGASSI	You love tennis
AGATHA	A wonderful name for big females, Saint Bernards, black-and-tan coonhounds, borzois
AGATHA CHRISTIE	A sneaky pet . . . good at puzzles
AGENT 99	Pair with Maxwell Smart
AGGIE	Nickname of Agnes
AGNES	Sounds so downtrodden. But, so great for a cat
AGNEW	An American fox terrier . . . feisty and a scrapper
AHAB	Wicked king of Israel . . . husband of Jezebel
AHMED	An Arabic name . . . a Sloughi is directly descended from royal Egyptian dogs . . . docile, obedient and affectionate
AIDA	You love opera
AIR BAG	A car salesman's pet
AIR JORDAN	Michael Jordan . . . basketball
AIRBORNE	A pilot's pet

AJAX	A cleaning fanatic's pet
AKBAR	Afghan hounds, ancient breed . . . courageous, sweet, and intelligent
AKIKO	Japanese bobtails or Japanese spitz
AKIMBO	Means, basically, bowlegged . . . it has to be an English bulldog, Pugs, ducks
AL	You're very close
AL CAPONE	My grandparents bought his house when they came to America
ALABAMA	A sexy southern belle
ALADDIN	It came with a lamp
ALBA	Albacore's nickname
ALBACORE	Tuna . . . great name for a fish or cat
ALBEE	Perfect for a wolf
ALBERT	Royalty . . . for a truly regal animal and a prince of a pet
ALBERTA	Royalty . . . for a truly regal female animal
ALBERTO	For a truly regal pet that uses hair products
ALCOTT	You love Louisa May
ALDEN	Calico long-haired Scottish folds . . . placid and adorable
ALDO	It brings a Ray of sunshine into your life
ALEX	Good name for a Great Dane
ALEXANDER	For a more formal Great Dane
ALEXANDER THE GREAT	For an exceptional Great Dane
ALEXI	Russian wolfhounds
ALF	He was once the rage of TV
ALFALFA	Also once the rage of TV . . . ran around with Buckwheat in *The Little Rascals* in 1954
ALFONSE	You have a snooty pet

ALFONSO	Your Spanish mastiff thinks of itself as a deposed king . . . walks around slightly depressed
ALFRED	Batman's butler, great for a superhero's sidekick
ALFREDO	A pasta lover's pet
ALGEBRA	A mathematician's pet
ALI	Usually for a cat . . . nice for Yorkshire terriers too
ALI BABA	The poor woodcutter in *The Arabian Nights*
ALI CAT	Strays
ALIAS	A criminal's pet
ALIBI	A liar's pet
ALICE B. TOKLAS	Your pet is partial to brownies
ALIEN	Devon rex, Cornish rex, sphynx . . . all hairless cats . . . then, you have the Chinese crested dog, also hairless
ALIMONY	A disgruntled divorcee's pet
ALISTER	Must be a good Cook . . . pair with Abe
ALIWISHES	Whatever Ali wants, Ali gets
ALKA-SELTZER	Your pet drives you crazy either by barking too much or missing the litter box too often
ALLENDALE	A Florida pet
ALLERGY	Good for a shedding animal
ALMA	Another perfect animal name. Large or small, ugly or cute, it fits
ALOHA	You have a thing for Hawaii
ALONSO	Good for a tomcat perhaps
ALONZO	Another one for basketball fans
ALTHEA	Lovely for a pretty golden Persian, Himalayan, or anything fluffy
ALVA	Good for a non-fluffy pet . . . short hair and muscular . . . bulldogs, beagles, German short-haired pointers

ALVIN	A chipmunk or a dancer's name
AMADEUS	For a very intense, preferably musically inclined, pet
AMAGANSETT	You like to be reminded of the Hamptons
AMANDA	American curl longhairs, beagles, fish
AMARETTO	Blue-mitted ragdolls or your typical alcoholic-reference pet, the Saint Bernard
AMARYLLIS	Triple with Peonie & Tulip
AMAZON	BIG, BEAUTIFUL, and FEMALE
AMBASSADOR	Your pet likes to greet visitors
AMBER	An exotic shorthair red spotted tabby (cats can certainly have very long names)
AMBROSE	One of my favorites. Good for nearly any animal
AMBROSIA	One of my favorite desserts
AMELDA	Four paws is a good start for a shoe collection
AMELIA	Birds
AMEN	A minister's pet
AMERICA	A patriot's pet
AMERICAN EXPRESS	For a patriot that likes to charge
AMETHYST	For your gem
AMIGO	You really consider it a friend
AMNESIA	A forgetful person's pet
AMOROUS	A gigolo's pet
AMOS	If your name is Andy
AMPLIFIER	Parrots, mynah birds, macaws, etc.
AMSTEL	Good for a lite pet
AMTRAK	Good for a fast pet
AMY	My friend Joan's dog and my friend Eva's daughter
ANALYST	A stockbroker's or a psychiatrist's pet

ANASTASIA	It makes me think of 'amnesia,' which I will now add to the list
ANCHORS AWEIGH	Good for a fish OR a pet for a sailor
ANCHOVY	For a fish, if you have a cat
ANDORA	For a nice, big torbie and white Maine coon
ANDRE	French bulldogs . . . or . . . tennis is your game
ANDREA	I met Andrea in ninth grade and we've been friends ever since. She lives in New Hampshire now
ANDY	What a name for a ragdoll!!! (that is a breed of cat . . . and one that I happen to own, too)
ANDY HARDY	For a sweet, open-faced, guileless pet
ANGEL	Well, at first aren't they all? You know best if it applies
ANGELICA	A pet from Houston
ANGELO	Italian pointers . . . elegant, thoughtful, loyal, and not very cheerful
ANGUS	OK. So, it's a great name for a bull. But, think of an Irish setter or an Irish wolfhound
ANITA	An up-hill pet
ANN MARGRET	Beautiful redhead . . . golden retrievers, Irish setters
ANN TAYLOR	For a pet that likes traditional dress, good shoes, and a good job
ANNE OF CLEVES	Pair with Henry VIII
ANNETTE	Great for a poodle . . . or . . . someone who liked the Mouseketeers
ANNIE	A very nice, basic name for any animal
ANNIE GET YOUR GUN	For someone who lives with PMS

ANNIE HALL	For a pet with long, straight hair, who is a bit confused, probably doesn't work, and is partial to sunglasses (pair with Ann Taylor)
ANNIE OAKLEY	You like to ride western
ANSEL	A photographer's pet
ANTHONY	Pair with Agnes
ANTIGONE	Oedipus's daughter
ANTOINE	A longhaired dachshund . . . I think it's a hysterical combination (but, I'm always my best audience)
ANTOINETTE	A female longhaired dachshund
ANTON	French bulldogs
ANTONIO	Wirehaired dachshunds . . . (almost as hysterical as Antoine)
ANTONY	A pet for a Marc . . . pair with Cleopatra
APACHE	A Southwestern pet
APERTURE	A photographer's pet
APHRODITE	A Greek goddess . . . any pet you think is gorgeous
APOLLO	The Greek god of music, poetry, prophecy, and medicine . . . wonderful for big, powerful animals
APPLE BROWN BETTY	American shorthair brown classic tabbies
APPLE PIE	American shorthair red classic tabbies
APPLEBY	American longhair white classic tabbies
APPLESAUCE	A mixture
APPYDAZE	You're so glad you got it
APRICOT	My favorite jam . . . and good for any orange- or red-colored pets
AQUARIUS	A January baby
AQUAVIT	A 100 proof baby
ARABELLA	Egyptian maus or a Himalayan cream point

ARABESQUE	A pet with elaborately decorative markings
ARABIAN KNIGHT	Either for a horse or a big, beautiful animal like a Russian wolfhound, Irish wolfhound, etc.
ARAFAT	Dobermans, German shepherds, Rottweilers, or very bossy parrots
ARAMIS	Your pet smells good
ARBERRY	Universal . . . cats, dogs, birds, gerbils
ARCHER	Someone good with a bow and arrow
ARCHIBALD	Great, strong name . . . perhaps bloodhounds, Great Danes, or Great Pyrenees
ARCHIE	A pet for a Betty, Veronica, or Jughead
ARCHIMEDES	Dalmatians
ARDEN	Your pet has great skin
ARETHA	Great schnauzers would certainly get a 'little respect'
ARF	For a silent dog
ARGYLE	Definitely for a tortoise cat
ARI	Aristotle's nickname
ARIEL	A flyer's pet
ARISTOCAT	A feline aristocrat
ARISTOCRAT	Afghans . . . regal and dignified
ARISTOPHANES	You have a dramatic pet
ARISTOTLE	Ari's full name. A bulldog would be very good, as would a boxer
ARIZONA	Another one for those who have southwestern preferences
ARLENE	Perfect for a beagle. Don't ask me why
ARLINGTON	For a national-minded pet
ARLO GUTHRIE	American foxhounds
ARMAND	Very international, sophisticated name
ARMANI	Italian pointers into clothes, of course
ARMORY	Another guard dog name

ARMSTRONG   You have strong arms . . . or . . . a linoleum floor

ARMY   It would have to be a bald bet, an archer's pet, and, perhaps, a French bulldog or a Devon rex

ARNOLD   I can only think of Schwarzenegger when I see that name now. But, it would be great for a basset hound

ARPEGE   A perfumed pet

ARPEL   A designer pet

ARROW   Dachshunds . . . straight and narrow

ARSENIO   A pet for a night owl

ART DECO   For anyone partial to the '40s

ARTHUR   Legendary king of England who led the Knights of the Round Table . . . also, my college sweetheart

ARTURO   For an Italian greyhound . . . loves peaceful people but frightened of children

ARTURO TOSCANINI   A Spinone Italiano. A very cute, wiry, big dog from France. But, the Italiano part went with the Arturo.

ARUBA   Good swimming name . . . fish, turtles, frogs

ASCOT   You hate ties

ASH   Any gray-colored animal

ASHLEY   Rhett and Scarlett were partial to him . . . in their own ways (nice for a triple)

ASHTON   Old English sheepdogs or pulis

ASIA   Nice name for a Chinese shar-pei (the wrinkled dog)

ASIMOV   For someone into science fiction

ASKHIM   When you want to know who made the poop in the living room . . . Askhim

ASPARAGUS   Any of your green varieties

ASPEN   A skier's pet

ASTA	The wirehaired terrier from "The Thin Man" series
ASTAIRE	Pair with Rogers
ASTRO	You loved *The Jetsons*
ATHENA	The goddess of wisdom, skills, and warfare. Any pet would be proud to have this name
ATHENS	The capital of Greece . . . so . . . A Greek hound, found only in Greece . . . lively and has a good sense of smell
ATLANTA	Capital of Georgia . . . a southern pet
ATLANTIS	Legendary island in Atlantic, west of Gibraltar, said to have sunk . . . doesn't bode well
ATLAS	BIG STRONG MALE
ATTILA	You have a Hun
AUDIT	An IRS agent or an accountant's pet
AUGIE	This definitely sounds like a mixed breed
AUGUSTUS	If you like the time of the Roman emperor Augustus . . . 63 B.C.–A.D. 14
AULD LANG SYNE	For a pet you get for old times' sake
AUNT JEMIMA	A nice, big, fat mamma! Newfoundland or Saint Bernard would be adorable
AUNTIE	A nurturing pet. A Newfoundland. Again
AUNTIE EM	I like this for bigger breeds, though it works for minis too
AUNTIE MAME	A pet that never stays put
AURELIA	Lakeland terriers . . . affectionate, spirited and tenacious
AURORA	For a star gazer . . . or . . . a bore
AUSSIE	An Australian animal . . . koalas
AUSTIN	Another Texas pet
AUTHOR	A writer's pet
AUTUMN	Your pet sheds

AVALON	A pet for a Frankie . . . or . . . an Annette
AVANTI	Someone always in a hurry's pet
AVENGER	What a name for a guard dog! Rottweiler, German shepherds, pit bulls, etc.
AVERY	Murphy Brown's boy
AVIS	A pet for someone in the car rental business
AVON	A pet for someone in the skin product business
AXL	For a pet with tattoos, or, shall we say, markings
AXLE	Your pet chases cars
AYATOLLAH	Pit bulls or any other pets you're afraid to talk back to
AZALEA	A landscape architect's pet
AZTEC	Your pet likes to build things
AZURE	Skye terriers

B-12	The pet really perks you up
B-2	A bird, or a bomber
BABBITT	The rabbit
BABE	You love baseball . . . or . . . you are very cool
BABE RUTH	You plan to play ball with it
BABETTE	A cook's pet . . . you enjoy a feast
BABY	Another thing to 'bring up'
BABY DEE	For a baby deerhound
BACALL	Bogie's baby . . . for a *Casablanca* fan
BACCARAT	For an absolutely crystal clear pet
BACH	A musician's pet
BACKGAMMON	You're a game player
BACON	Your pet has high cholesterol
BADGES	You aspire to law enforcement
BAGEL	Triple with . . . Baguette & Bialy
BAGUETTE	French poodles, or, perhaps, dachshunds (long and narrow)
BAILEY	Double with Barnum
BAKER	You have a sweet tooth

BAKLAVA	For a sweet little Greek pet
BALD ED	One for the hairless breeds
BALLERINA	Adorable for a bulldog
BALLY	You're into good shoes
BALLYHOO	For the adventurous pet
BALTHUS	20th-century artist . . . good for a beefy kind of pet
BALUGA	A pet with a taste for the finer things in life
BALZAC	Behind every great fortune there is a crime
BAMBI	For a deer pet
BAMM BAMM	You love the Flinstones
BANANA BREAD	For a monkey or any primate without a movable thumb
BANDIT	Smokey's pal
BANDITT	Your pet loves to steal your clothing
BANKER	You have a pet pig
BARBARA ANN	Sheep . . . bah, bah, bah, bah Barbara Ann
BARBARELLA	Sorry, Jane
BARKER	If he's loud, has his own game show, and can't keep his paws to himself
BARLEY	Your pet likes soup
BARNABY	Perfect for a bloodhound
BARNABY JONES	A police dog . . . or . . . a basset hound whose specialty is hunting
BARNETT	The name of a dentist I know that does root canal for a living (YUCH!!!)
BARNEY	Your child only wants a purple dinosaur
BARNUM	Pair with Bailey
BARON	A pet with no hair
BARONESS	For a very feminine and regal pet . . . with no hair

BARRIO BOY	A pet from upper Manhattan
BARRY	My insurance agent
BARTHOLOMEW	Bartholomew for a cat
BARTHOLOMOO	Bartholomew for a cow
BARTLEBY	English setters, English bulldogs . . . or fuzzy, furry cats
BARTOK	You love classical music
BASHA	For a Lhasa Apso, Shih Tzu, Maltese, Pekingese
BASIL	For a pet that adds a little spice to your life
BASS MAN	A pet with a low growl
BASTILLE	For a pet you retrieve from the humane society
BATMAN	Double with Robin
BAXTER	Shorthaired Saint Bernards
BAYOU	American bloodhounds
BAZAAR	A strange, yet fashionable, pet
BAZOOKA JOE	Perfect for a blowfish
BEA	A very homey, cozy name . . . something solid about it
BEACH BOY	A pet that can catch a frisbee and chug a beer at the same time
BEANS	Brown California Spangleds, Yorkies
BEANSTALK	Tortoiseshell British shorthairs, or very tall animals, or climbing animals
BEAR	For a big cuddly animal, or one with no hair
BEARDSLEY	Old English Sheepdogs
BEARNAISE	For a pup that likes a little sauce on his T-bone
BEASTIE BOY	Deutsche dogges, or any other large guard-dog type
BEATRICE	For a little princess
BEAU	A male pet for a female owner

BEAUCHAMP	Pronounced 'Beecham'—great shopping street in London
BEAVER	Ward & June's son
BECKER	I know you know Boris, but do you remember Sandy?
BEDOUIN	Your pet just can't stay in one place
BEDROCK	Fred Flintstone's hometown
BEEFEATER	Harlequin Great Dane . . . REAL beef eaters
BEAKER	A character on *Muppet Babies*
BEETHOVEN	Your pet is hard of hearing
BEEZER	John VanBiesbrouck
BEEZNEEZ	You think it's the GREATEST
BEGUILER	The pet whose eyes can talk you into anything
BEIGE	For a beige pet
BELDING	For *Saved by the Bell* fans
BELLA	For a pretty Italian pet
BELLE	For a pretty French pet
BELLOW	For a loud American pet
BEN	For a gentle pet
BEN HUR	You always wanted to drive a chariot
BENITO	Italian pointers, parrots, mynah birds
BENJI	Wirehair fox terriers
BENJIE	Same
BENNY	Small, gentle pets
BENO	Nice, sweet name . . . not to be confused with the gas medication Beano
BENSON	A pet that serves you
BENTLEY	For the Rolls Royce of pets
BENTLY	Same
BERKELEY	You have a radical pet
BERMUDA	Tropical fish
BERNADETTE	Vizslas . . . intelligent, obedient, exceptional sense of smell

BERNADINE	Airedales, Swedish dachsbrackes, or small Swiss hounds
BERNIE	An old pet that smokes cigars and goes to the track
BERRY	A pet for a Chuck
BERT	Pair with Ernie
BERTHA	For the biggest puppy in the litter
BERTIE	Goes to the track with Bernie
BERTRAM	Bearded collies . . . a herding breed, with a joyous and affectionate personality
BESSIE	What else?
BETAMAX	For a pet that will soon be replaced
BETH	For a *Rockford* aficionado
BETSEY	Sounds like an active cat
BETSY	A dog with difficulty house breaking . . . (Betsy Wetsey?)
BETTE DAVIS EYES	Pugs or cocker spaniels
BETTINA	Lapphunds . . . a Swedish dog, affectionate, patient with children and distrustful of strangers
BETTY BOOP	For a Maltese . . . nice big eyes
BEULAH	TV show of the same name, 1950–53
BEVERLY	For a cat that likes to sit on sills
BIALY	See Bagel
BIANCA	My children's great-grandmother . . . great name
BIDDY	For a small card-playing pet
BIG BELLY	A basset hound who enjoys food just a little too much
BIG BERTHA	For any of your oversized breeds
BIG BETTY	For any pet that works the counter at a truck stop
BIG BILL	For a very expensive breed
BIG BIRD	Yellow parakeets
BIG EAR BOB	A rabbit name

BIG EASY	For a mush
BIG MAC	Any large, imposing animal . . . or . . . quite the opposite, small and petite
BIG SHOT	A pet with a Napoleon complex
BIG TONY	For a pet that makes you an offer you can't refuse
BIJAN	By appointment only
BILL	My ex-husband
BILL BAILEY	Won't you come home . . . your pet keeps wandering
BILL HICKOK	A pet that's always ready to be wild
BILLIE JEAN	Retrievers . . . any pet that goes after tennis balls
BILLMAR	Bichon avaneses, Labrador retrievers, Chesapeake Bay retrievers
BILLOW	Fluffy cats
BILLY DEE	Border collies
BING	Crooners
BINGO	There was a farmer . . .
BINKI	Toy fox terriers, Yorkshire terriers, toy poodles, etc.
BINZER	Yugoslavian mountain hounds
BIONIC	For a very strong pet
BIRD DOG	For your hunting breeds
BIRDIE	A golfer's pet
BISCUIT	Race horses and parrots
BISHOP	A chess player's pet
BISQUE	Fish
BIXLER	My ex-boss
BJ	Basenjis
BJORN	A tennis player's pet
BLACK BEANS	Pets with a lot of gas
BLACK FOOT	Any pet with black paws
BLACK JACK	A gambler's pet . . . or . . . a black Jack Russell terrier
BLACK MOON	A black pet with a white face

BLACK RUSSIAN	For a black pet with a taste for vodka
BLACK SMOKE	Black smoke Asians
BLACKBERRY	A black pet with a taste for fruit
BLACKFOOT	See BLACK FOOT . . . same, different spelling
BLACKWELL	Your pet has discerning taste in clothing
BLANCH	You have a white pet and love *Golden Girls*
BLANCHE	A *Streetcar* fan
BLANKET	For a lapcat
BLARNEY	Your pet never tells the truth
BLEDSOE	Chocolate-shaded American shorthairs
BLOCKER	A Rottweiler . . . not too easy to get by him
BLONDIE	Dagwood's wife, Blondie Bumstead
BLOOD BROTHER	For someone that feels a very special affinity to their pet
BLOOM	In Love
BLOOMER	For a puppy with enormous paws
BLOSSOM	I love this name for a pet
BLU	I love this name too
BLUE	This one too
BLUE CHEESE	This, however, makes me break out
BLUE CHIP	A stock market investor's pet
BLUE MOON	You saw it standing alone . . . without a dream in its heart, without a love of its own
BLUEBELL	Any pet that's delicate and feminine
BLUEBERRY	For a 60's person who found his thrill on the hill
BO DIDDLEY	For a 60's person who liked Bo Diddley
BO JACKSON	Big dogs that run fast
BOB	American shorthair tabbies, beagles, Airedales
BOBBSEY	For twins

BOBBY BROWN	For any pet that likes rap
BOBBY DARIN	For anyone who learned to dance to "Mack the Knife" (see Mack the Knife)
BOBBY HULL	You love hockey
BOBBY SHORT	Bulldogs . . . perfection
BOCA	For a parrot with a big mouth
BODYGUARD	For a Yorkie or a Doberman or a Costner . . . whichever you fancy
BOGART	For a *Casablanca* fan. Pair with Bacall
BOGATTI	For a foreign car enthusiast
BOGGS	For an animal that boggles the mind
BOGIE	And Bacall
BOIS DE BOULOGNE	You love France
BOJANGLES	For a Mister
BOLSHOI	Ballerina's big brother
BOLT	Your pet keeps running away
BONBON	It has to be for a sweet little French poodle
BOND . . . JAMES BOND	English foxhounds
BONE A PART	Dogs with jaws big enough to take the bone apart . . . get it?!
BONJOVI	A singer's pet
BONNIE	Irish setters, Irish terriers, etc.
BONNIE LASS	Also for any of the Irish breeds
BONO	Your pet sings like a dream
BONSAI	For a dwarf pet
BOO	Someone I went to high school with . . . a pet that startles easily
BOOKER	A casting agent's pet
BOOMER	A pet for someone born between 1946 and 1964
BOOTS	Boots is for dogs and Socks is for cats
BOOTSIE	If Socks is for cats and Boots is for dogs, then Bootsie is for a wussy dog

BORAX	You love to clean
BOREALIS	For star gazers
BORG	Tennis anyone?
BORGIA	Lucrezia
BORIS	For any of the Russian breeds . . . wolfhound, borzoi, etc.
BORIS BADENOV	Pair with Natasha Fatale
BORSCHT	Again, Russian wolfhounds, borzois, Russian blues
BOSCO	The favorite syrup for making chocolate milk in the '50s and '60s
BOSH	Small Continental spaniels, parakeets, turtles
BOSLEY	A *Charlie's Angels* fan
BOSS	A Springsteen fan
BOSWELL	Rough-coated Bohemian pointers . . . a hunting dog from Bohemia . . . and aristocratic to boot
BOTTICELLI	For a fleshy pet
BOUILLABAISSE	A good name for the entire fish tank
BOUNCER	Pugs or Yorkshire terriers, Rottweilers, or Dobermans
BOURGUIGNON	Your pet is a French meat eater
BOWERY BOY	One of my favorite TV shows growing up
BOWSER	Bloodhounds
BOXER	Any pet that comes home with a few too many bruises
BOXY	Scottish terriers, West Highland terriers
BOY SCOUT	For goody-goodies
BOY WONDER	For a Robin
BOYCHICK	For one of those Easter chicks that you eventually have to give away once they start cock-a-doodling
BOYD	For a bichon frise

BOZETTE   Bozo's girlfriend

BOZO   Bozette's boyfriend

BOZWELL   Maltese, cockapoos, or Oriental reds

BRADLEY   Terriers, cocker spaniels, English springer spaniels

BRAHMS   Your pet sleeps a lot

BRANCUSI   French hounds . . . vivacious, robust hunters

BRANDO   Your pet knows how to tango

BRANDON   *90210*

BRANDY   There are an awful lot of Brandys. I don't know why

BRAWLER   Boxer's compadre

BRENDON   Not quite *90210*. This name literally means 'stinking hair' . . . I find that very interesting

BRIDGE   For a pet that makes peace in the family

BRIDIE   Irish setters, Irish terriers, or Irish water spaniels

BRIE   My friends Sunny & Brad's standard poodle. Pair with Baguette

BRIDGETTE   Loves Bernie

BRILLIANT   Very colorful pets

BRINKER   For a Brink's truck guard

BRINKS   Guard dogs

BRIOCHE   You love breakfast

BRISTLE   For a prickly pet

BROADHURST   A theatergoer's pet

BROADWAY JOE   For a Sunday quarterback

BRODERICK   Old English sheepdogs

BRODIE   A pet in its prime (Miss Jean)

BROKER   An insurance agent's pet

BROMLEY   A skier's pet

BRONCO   For your larger breeds

BRONSON   For someone who knows how to take care of his family

BRONTË	*Jane Eyre* is one of your favorites
BROOKS	Our Miss
BROTHER LOVE	You're into wrestling
BROWN SUGAR	Brown classic tabbies, chocolate Labs
BROWNIE	One of the all-time favorite pet names (not necessarily mine)
BROWNING	For a pet that's not quite toast yet
BROWSER	Your pet likes to window shop
BRUCE	A very pensive goldfish
BRUNHILDA	For a real work dog . . . or . . . a Wagner lover
BRUNO	German wirehair pointers
BRUTUS	A pet that you feel might eventually, and surprisingly, betray you
BRYANT	For a pet that gumbles, uh, grumbles
BRYNNER	You have a bald pet with a good sense of drama
BUBBA	A bullmastiff linebacker
BUBBLES	Another fish name
BUBELEH	Yiddish for sweetheart
BUBKAS	Yiddish for peanuts
BUCCELLATI	You love jewelry
BUCKINGHAM	English bulldogs, English springer spaniels
BUCKSHOT	For a gun lobbyist
BUCKWHEAT	A pet with hair that stands straight up (Cane Nudo)
BUDDY	Sally's pal from *The Dick Van Dyke Show*
BUFFALO BILL	A pet that just can't seem to win the Super Bowl
BUFFALO BOB	*Howdy Doody* pal
BUFFET	Your pet eats constantly
BUFFY	From the show *Family Affair*
BUGS	Bunnies
BUGSY	You identified with the movie

BULFINCH	You're into mythology
BULGARI	You love jewelry and don't mind overpaying
BULLET	The Wonder Dog . . . Roy Rogers
BULLWINKLE	You have a moose . . . or pair with Rocket J. Squirrel
BUMPERS	For a dog that catches the car and hits the bumpers
BUMSTEAD	For Blondie and Dagwood fans
BUNKO	For someone into fraud
BUNNY	Chinchilla Persians, rabbits
BUNYAN	You either love Paul or you have problem feet
BURBANK	Your pet loves to watch game shows
BURGESS	Beagles
BUSTER	For a Crab or a Brown
BUSTER BROWN	Your pet loves to get into your shoes
BUTCH	For a sexually ambivalent pet
BUTCH CASSIDY	For someone into cowboys or bank and train robberies
BUTLER	He, definitely, did it
BUTTER	Cream point Himalayans
BUTTERBALL	You got a turkey
BUTTERCUP	A female bulldog
BUTTERSCOTCH	Golden Persians
BUTTON	A pet with one spot on it
BUTTONS	Dalmatians
BUZZ OFF	Guard dogs
BUZZIE	*Leave it to Beaver*
BUZZY	A drinker's pet
BYBLOS	For a blue Tonkinese into good clothing
BYRD	Birds (A Robin if you're a New Yorker)
BYRON	A pet that has a sense of intellectual superiority

C. S. LEWIS	You love literature
C3PO	You love *Star Wars*
CAB	You love taxis
CABALLERO	You love Spanish cowboys
CABBAGE PATCH	You love Cabbage Patch dolls
CABBAGE ROSE	You love flowers
CABBIE	You might not love New York, but it's definitely a New Yorker's pet
CABERNET	You love red
CABIN FEVER	For an indoor pet
CABLE	You love television
CABOT	Wirehaired pointing griffons . . . so cute, wiry, lively, tallish, and intelligent
CABOT COVE	You love *Murder She Wrote*
CAESAR	You love salad
CAFÉ AU LAIT	For a black and white
CAGNEY	You're a James fan
CAINE	Kung Fu is your game
CAIRO	Pharaoh Hounds, salukis
CAKE	Bichon Frises

CALAMITY JANE	You have a very clumsy pet
CALCULATOR	A very cunning pet
CALDER	A painter's pet
CALDWELL	Another one for art lovers
CALEB	Bronze Egyptian maus
CALENDAR GIRL	For a pinup pet
CALHOUN	Irish setters, Irish wolfhounds, Irish terriers
CALI	Blue classic tabbies or British shorthairs
CALIFORNIA DREAMER	You're a displaced Californian
CALLAHAN	Another one for all the Irish breeds
CALLIE	Callahan's nickname
CALLOWAY	You love jazz
CALVIN	You have an English sheepdog or you love cotton underwear
CALZONE	You love Italian food
CAMBER	Iceland dogs . . . lively, active, and like to eat fish
CAMBRIDGE	For an Anglophile or a Harvard grad
CAMDEN	Norwich terriers . . . one of the smallest terriers
CAMELLA	A pet unfaithful to its mate
CAMELOT	You loved the '60s
CAMERA	A photographer's pet
CAMARO	For a Chevy fan
CAMARON	Always makes me think of Swazey
CAMI	Norwegian elkhounds . . . specialize in hunting elk
CAMILLE	Your pet is very dramatic
CAMP	For a pet that's really "in"
CAMPAIGN	A political pet
CAMPBELL	You like canned soup, "Soap", or Andy Warhol
CAMPER	It's an outdoorsy pet
CAMUS	It's an intellectual pet

CANCEL	It's an angry pet
CANDICE	It's a Murphy pet
CANDIDE	Voltaire's novel has left an impression on you
CANDY	It's a sweet pet
CANNES	It's a movie critic's pet
CANON	It's a copy cat
CAP D'ANTIBES	You love the south of France
CAPER	For a James Bondian pet
CAPONE	Your pet knows how to keep the neighbors in check
CAPOTE	It's a true man pet
CAPPUCCINO	It's an Italian hyperactive pet
CAPPY	Bedlington terriers
CAPRA	You love romantic comedies
CAPTAIN	For a courageous pet
CAPTAIN CAT	It's going to be a very big one
CAPTAIN HOOK	Three-legged pets
CAPTAIN KANGAROO	You had kids in the '70s
CAPTAIN VIDEO	You had kids in the '50s
CAR 54	You seem to always be saying "WHERE ARE YOU?"
CARAMEL	Cream classic tabbies
CARAMEL CUSTARD	Cream classic tabbies and whites
CARBONARA	Saucy pets
CARL	Carl the Rottweiler of children's book fame
CARLISLE	For someone who sells clothing from their home
CARLITO	Your pet likes to get his way
CARLOS	For a French poodle (if you're in the mood to be hilarious)
CARLOTTA	I once stayed in a villa in Tuscany named Carlotta. It was in shocking condition . . . and I left quickly

CARLTON	A smoker's pet
CARLY	Cats that love to sing and write songs
CARMEL	A California dreamer
CARMEN	You love opera
CARMICHAEL	You love hoagies
CARMINE	You love Italian restaurants
CARNATION	Another for the flowery pets
CARNEGIE	Your pet will be sleeping in the hall
CAROL	"Oh, Carol" . . . you made a mistake
CARPOOL	For any suburban parent
CARRERA	You like sunglasses
CARRINGTON	A pet for a *Dynasty* fan
CARSON	You miss Johnny
CARSTAIRS	A butler wanna-be
CARTER	You have a pet with lust
CARTIER	For a jewel of a pet
CARTOUCHE	Silver Egyptian Maus
CARTWRIGHT	A pet for anyone named Adam, Hos, L'il Joe, or Pa
CARUSO	Your pet has big lungs and a need to sing
CASABLANCA	Your pet will live in a white house
CASBAH	For a 'rockin' pet
CASEY	American shorthairs
CASHMERE	Soft, furry pets
CASINO	A gambler's pet
CASPER	For a vanishing dog
CASPURR	For a vanishing cat
CASSANDRA	Very fancy, fluffy Persian cats
CASSATT	American impressionist
CASSIDY	For any animal that hops along
CASSIE	For an American shorthair (or longhair)
CASSIUS	For a pet with feet of clay
CASTRO	For a dictatorial pet
CAT	Either you're a lazy namer or a fan of *Breakfast at Tiffany's*

CATALINE	You're a creative namer
CATASAQUA	For a cat of Indian descent
CAVIAR	Persian cats, fish
CB	You don't have a car phone yet
CBS	You're partial to Westinghouse
CD	You've given away all your tapes
CECIL	English springer spaniels, English bulldogs, English sheepdogs
CECILIA	For a pet who's "breakin' your heart"
CEDRIC	I love this name
CEE CEE	For seeing-eye dogs
CELESTE	For a heavenly pet
CELIA	You're getting a seal
CELLO	For a big, fat, oversized pet
CENTRAL	The second elementary school I went to. I went to three. Chatsworth, Central, and F. E. Bellows
CERUTTI	Fine children's clothes
C'EST LA VIE	You're not thrilled, but you're resigned to keeping it
CEZANNE	A painter's pet
CHA CHA	Your pet dances
CHACHI	*Happy Days*
CHAGALL	Your pet loves looking out the windows
CHAM-PU	You need a name that begins with C
CHAMBERLAIN	English bulldogs
CHAMP	Boxers and bulldogs
CHAMPAGNE	You got a bubbly one
CHAMPAIGN	A political animal
CHANCALOT	Your cat thinks it has more than nine lives
CHANCELLOR	A diplomatic pet
CHANEL	Your pet smells good and dresses well
CHANG	Tibetan terriers, or Chinese temple dogs, Lhasa Apsos
CHANNEL	You live for the remote control
CHANNING	A skinny pet with big lips and a loud voice

CHAPSTICK	For someone named Susie . . . or . . . someone with problem lips
CHARCOAL	Any smoky-colored pet
CHARDONNAY	Kathy Lee's bichon
CHARGER	You have a horse or a shopaholic
CHARLA	Chestnut Angoras
CHARLEMAGNE	French pointers
CHARLES	Formal (see 'Chuck')
CHARLES IN CHARGE	Your Charles is a very bossy boy
CHARLEY	American bloodhounds
CHARLIE	You love Peanuts
CHARLIE BROWN	Pair with Snoopy
CHARLIE CHAN	For a Chinese crested dog detective
CHARLIE'S ANGEL	An angel for a Charlie
CHARLOTTE	Either you got a spider or your home is crowded with webs
CHARMER	Your pet is a Don Juan
CHARMING	For a prince
CHARMSIE	For a princess
CHARO	For busty song birds
CHASE	Your dog runs after cars
CHASER	American impressionist
CHATSWORTH	The first elementary school I went to. Also Jack Benny's chauffeur. I love this name
CHATZUK	Cinnamon Javaneses
CHAUCER	English setters, English bulldogs, or English springer spaniels
CHAUNCEY	Irish blue terriers, Irish setters, or Irish water spaniels
CHAUNCY	Same
CHECKERS	See Nixon
CHEERIOS	My favorite evening snack . . . nice crunch and not too fattening

CHEERS	You live in Boston, and don't mind a drink now and then
CHEESECAKE	It would be my favorite evening snack if it weren't so fattening
CHEESER	For a pinup pet
CHEEVER	For an under or an over
CHEKHOV	Russian wolfhounds, borzois, Russian blues
CHELSEA	Old English sheepdogs, Yorkshire terriers, English bulldogs
CHELSEY	Torties and white Scottish folds
CHER	For a multitalented pet with a predilection to dressing way out there
CHEROKEE	You're partial to Indian names
CHESSIE	Chesapeake Bay retrievers
CHESTER	Actually, someone I wanted to go out with and never did
CHESTNUT	For a horse. Also, my hair color (the actual name of the color . . . on the bottle)
CHEWBACCA	*Star Wars*
CHEYENNE	My grandmother and I used to watch this TV western together (now there was someone to go out with)
CHI CHI	Little, teeny-weeny pets
CHICO	My childhood dog's name. I bought him for $14 at the local pet store. I had to borrow half of it from my best friend Andrea
CHIEF	Giant schnauzers . . . large, steady watchdog and bodyguard
CHIFFON	Blue-cream point Himalayans
CHILI	For a hot pet
CHILI PEPPER	Any of the red breeds
CHILL	For a hyper pet
CHIPPER	A happy pet
CHLOE	A designer's pet
CHOCK FULL O'NUTS	You have a lunatic

CHOCOLATE	For a brown pet
CHOCOLATE CHIP	For a brown-and-black pet
CHOCOLATE MALT	For a brown-and-beige pet
CHOCOLATE MOUSSE	For a pudgy, soft, brown pet
CHOP SUEY	Any of the Asian breeds . . . Lhasa Apso, Shih Tzu, blue Tonkinese, etc.
CHOPIN	A musician's pet
CHOPPER	Your pet has big teeth
CHOPSTICK	You always insist on them, though you never quite get the food to your mouth
CHOU EN-LAI	Any of the Asian breeds
CHOW MEIN	Perfect for a Chow Chow
CHOWDER	You own a clam
CHRISTIE	Pair with Sotheby
CHROMIUM	You're on a diet
CHUCK	For an informal King Charles spaniel
CHUNK	A fat cat
CHURCHILL	A bulldog with a cigar
CHUTNEY	Golden Persians
CHUTZPAH	Your pet has no inhibitions
CINDERELLA	Swans
CINDERFELLA	You're a Jerry Lewis fan
CINDY	Cinderella's nickname
CINNAMON	Choice for the cinnamon Javanese
CISSY	Another name for those hard-to-housebreak pets
CLAIRE	One of the neighborhood children I baby-sat for. Now she's a psychiatrist and should be baby-sitting me
CLANCY	A police dog
CLAPTON	A guitarist's pet
CLARA	Bernese mountain dogs . . . very big, but energetic and loyal

CLARA BARTON	Your pet thinks it's a nurse . . . white pets
CLARABELL	Triple with Howdy Doody and Buffalo Bob
CLARENCE	Same
CLARISSA	Pet pigs or cows
CLARK	Pair with Lois
CLARK KENT	Your pet is a quick change artist
CLASSIC	A golfer's pet
CLAUDE	French spaniels
CLAUDIO	Italian pointers
CLAYTON	American Staffordshire terriers
CLEO	The bassett hound on *The People's Choice*
CLEOPATRA	For a pet that has total self-confidence and possibly a touch of grandiosity
CLERGY	A black cat with a white neck
CLIFF	A postman's pet
CLIFFORD	Weimaraners . . . affectionate and tend to be stubborn
CLIVE	For someone in the music business
CLOCKWORK ORANGE	For a very bazaar orange tabby
CLOONEY	A pet for a Rosemary
CLORIS	Mary Tyler Moore's neighbor
CLOROX	A bleached blonde's pet
CLOUD	For a very fluffy white cat
CLOVER	For a crimson pet
CLUE	For a game player
CLUELESS	Your pet's a little slow on the uptake
CLYDE	Pair with Bonnie
CO MO SHUN	It's a hyperactive addition to the family
COACH	An athlete's pet
COBRA	Pit bulls
COCHISE	Your pet wears feathers
COCKTAIL	Your pet comes to life after 5:00

COCO	Perfection for chocolate poodles or chocolate labs
CODY	A pet for a Kathy Lee fan
COKE	Pair with Pepsi
COLA	For a bubbly pet
COLETTE	French poodles, French bulldogs
COLLECTOR	For a pet that picks up strays and brings them home
COLLEEN	Irish setters, Irish terriers
COLLIN	Another one for all the Irish breeds
COLOMBO	Either you love yogurt . . . or . . . you have a sloppy-looking pet that never lets go of an idea
COLONEL KLINK	A pet for a *Hogan's Heroes* fan
COLONEL POTTER	A pet for a *M*A*S*H* fan
COLORADO	A skier's pet
COLT	For your larger, lean breeds . . . or it's your forty-fifth pet
COLUMBIA	A drug dealer's pet
COLUMBO	A detective's pet
COLUMBUS	An adventurous pet
COMANCHE	A wild pet
COMATOSE	A listless pet
COMBINATION	Mutts
COMPTON	A know-it-all
COMSTOCK	Basset hounds
CONCHITTA	Chihuahuas
CONDOR	Doberman pinschers
CONFETTI	Your pet was born on New Year's Eve
CONGO	African pets
CONGRESSMAN	A politician's pet
CONNECTICUT YANKEE	A pet from New England
CONNOR	Australian terriers
CONNORS	A Jimmy fan
CONRAD	Your pet will only stay at a Hilton

CONSTABLE	A serious pet that walks the grounds
CONSTANCE	His mate
CONSTANTINE	Greek pets
CONSUELA	Longhaired Saint Bernards, harlequin Great Danes
CONTESSA	You have a very fancy pet
CONWAY TWITTY	Your pet sings
COOPER	You like Gary
COORS	You like beer
COPACABANA	You were going to choose Rico but decided this was luckier
CORA	Smooth fox terriers, calicos, turtles
CORAL	Orange cats, fish, and gerbils
CORAZÓN	Heart, in Spanish
CORBETT	Great spitz
CORDUROY	A striped pet
CORINA	Blue and white Maine coons
CORRINA, CORRINA	I love you so
CORKY	For a Murphy Brown fan
CORNELIA	A female briard
CORNELIUS	A male briard . . . a wonderful name, actually. I like it for anything
CORNY	Your parrot tells bad jokes
COROT	Artist
CORPORATE	A pet for someone that works at IBM
CORTEZ	One very cool dude
CORY	A pet that likes to eat your leftovers
COSBY	Your pet is very funny
COSELL	You love sports
COSMO	You loved *Topper*
COSMOS	You love the planets
COSTA	A tough, manly pet
CÔTE D'AZUR	You love the south of France
COTTAGE CHEESE	Dieting is your way of life

COUNSELOR	You turn to it whenever you have problems
COUNT BASIE	A very mellow, contented animal
COUNTESS	Very regal pets
COUSTEAU	Your favorite fish
COWBOY	For a Jack Russell terrier with a bandana around his neck
COWGIRL	For a girl Jack Russell terrier with a bandana around her neck
CRACKER JACK	Another favorite name for the Jack Russell
CRACKERS	Either your pet has a screw loose . . . or . . . for Polly, of course
CRACKLIN' ROSE	For a very old, wrinkled Rose
CRAIG	Scottish terriers
CRAMER	Flat-coated retrievers . . . looks like a Newfoundland, obedient and affectionate
CRANBERRY	For a red squishy pet
CRAZY EDDIE	For a pet into electronics . . . that occasionally gets itself into big trouble
CREAM	The real thing
CREATOR	For a pet that creates havoc
CRÈME CARAMEL	Cream tabby point Devon rexes
CRÈME DE CACAO	Chocolate tortie Burmese, mini poodles
CREMORA	A substitute pet
CROCKETT	Coonhounds, Chesapeake Bay retrievers, or any of the hunting breeds
CROISSANT	French poodles, French bulldogs, French spaniels
CROMWELL	Gordon setters . . . Scottish, intelligent, and less active than other setters
CROUTON	A salad eater's pet
CRUISER	Definitely for a non-neutered male pet
CRUNCH	English bulldogs, boxers

CRUSADER	Your pet will talk you into doing exactly what you didn't want to do
CRUSADER RABBIT	Rabbits come to mind
CRYSTAL	A pet for a Carrington
CUCUMBER	Shorthaired dachshunds
CUDDLES	Old English sheepdog . . . unless, of course, snakes are your thing
CUJO	You're into Stephen King
CUPCAKE	Rottweilers, golden Persians, Welsh corgis, or whatever strikes your fancy
CUPID	A matchmaker's pet
CURLY	Triple with Moe and Larry
CUSTARD	A fat person's pet
CUSTER	Your pet is always fighting
CUSTER'S LAST STAND	The last of the last litter
CUTIE PIE	A bichon frise . . . what could be cuter?
CUTLER	Rough-coated collies. This is the *Lassie* dog. Robust, active and intelligent
CYRANO	Pets with long noses (Borzois come to mind), or dachsunds or parrots
CYRIL	Bassett hounds, parrots, fish

D A T	"Digital audio tape"—better recording than with a cassette tape.
D BLUE SEA	You listen to Debussy while sailing
D'ARTAGNAN	One of the Three Musketeers
D'MAN	A political pet
D'AMATO	A political pet
DADA	You were upset when your child said 'Mama' first
DAFFNEY	Blue-cream point Himalayans
DAFFODIL	Westphalian bassets, Scottish terriers, Chow Chows
DAFFY	You have a duck
DA GAMA	For someone that likes sailing the seven seas
DAGMAR	A Swedish elkhound, because I remember *I Remember Mama*
DAGWOOD	Pair with Blondie
DAILY DOUBLE	A gambler's pet
DAILY NEWS	A dog that's paper trained
DAILY TIMES	A discerning dog that's paper trained
DAISHI	A dashing Shih Tzu

DAISY	My own standard poodle . . . They are the most wonderful dogs
DAKOTA	For an Afghan with a cowboy scarf around her neck
DALE	You loved Roy Rogers
DALE EVANS	She loved him more
DALI	A painter's pet
DALLAS	You're either into cheerleaders or football
DAME	You have a tough broad pet
DAMIAN	Rottweilers, Deutsch dogges, Dobermans, etc.
DAMIEN	It's an omen and appears to be a pet from hell
DAMON	Boxers, great spitz, Pomeranians, turtles, fish
DAMSEL	Your pet is constantly in distress
DAN RIVER	It likes to sleep in your sheets
DANBURY	A pet from Connecticut
DANCER	A reindeer or a dancer
DANDEE	For a positively positive pet
DANDY	Dandie Dinmont terriers
DANDY DAN	You're into '60s music
DANETTE	A female Dan
DANIEL BOONE	You love coonskin hats
DANIELLE	A pet made of Steele
DANISH	A chubby pet
DANNY BOY	An Irish pet
DANTE	Doberman pinschers, Newfoundlands, snakes
DAPHNE	One of the very feminine names
DAPPER	You plan to keep it immaculately groomed
DARBERT	Norsk buhunds . . . Norwegian descent, courageous and energetic

DARBY	Irish blue terriers, Irish setters, Irish wolfhounds
DARE	You have a daredevil
DAREN	Bearded collies . . . very cute looking, fairly large, a lot of fun, and like to sleep outside
DARIA	You spent more than you should have on it
DARIAN LAMBERT	For a pet that knows how to make "tracks"
DARIEN	Another Connecticut pet
DARIN	Another spelling for the bearded collie
DARK CHOCOLATE	Any of your brown to black pets
DARLENE	You watched the Mouseketeers
DARLING	Peter Pan . . . Wendy's last name
DARNEL	Tennessee treeing brindles (that's a dog, really)
DARREN	*Bewitched*
DARRYL	Darryl's other brother
DARTER	A mouse in the house
DARTH VADER	A big black dog with a light saber
DARWIN	You have a monkey
DASH	Greyhounds, or other racing type of pets
DATA	For a computer buff
DATABASE	Your pet keeps track of the family
DATO	Japanese spitz . . . bold and happy, but suspicious of strangers
DAVIS	Any of the English breeds
DAVY	Any of the American breeds . . . also, parrots and gerbils
DAVY CROCKETT	Another one for a coonskin hat lover
DAWN	My middle name

DAY CARE	You don't plan to ever leave your pet home alone
DAYTONA BEACH	Car racing is your thing
DAZZLE	For a real crowd pleaser
DAZZY	For a pet with a far-off look in its eyes
DBX	For a sound aficionado
DC	A political pet
DD	See Dee Dee
DE NIRO	For someone that likes Robert
DEAN	For someone that likes school
DEANO	For someone that likes Dean Martin
DEBUSSY	For someone that likes music
DECKER	For someone that likes boxers
DECORATOR	For a pet that leaves new "items" around the house
DEE DEE	Dandie Dinmonts
DEEJAY	Your parrot is always talking
DEGAS	A painter's pet
DELBERT	Shorthaired dachshunds
DELIA	A card player's pet
DELICIA	For an Italian pet that loves to eat
DELICIOUS	For an American pet that loves to eat
DELILAH	A pet that's into grooming
DELLA	For a pet that likes to go out in the Street . . . or . . . that watches Perry Mason reruns with you
DELMAN	You have a shoe fetish
DELMONICO	For a person that likes the best hotels
DELMONTE	You will only feed it canned food
DELORES	A song my son wrote about 'Delores in the Forest'
DELTA	It's a bird (it's a plane)
DELTA BLUE	It's a blue bird
DELTA DAWN	It's an early bird

DEMERIT	You are always punishing it
DEMI	For someone who wants Moore
DEMITASSE	For any of the mini breeds
DEMITRI	Greek hounds
DEMITRIUS	Another Greek pet
DEMO	For a pet always having to prove itself
DEMOLITION MAN	For a big, clumsy pet
DEMPSEY	Another Jack Russell name . . . or a boxer
DENISE	Shubi doo, I'm in love with youoo Denise shubi doo
DENNIS THE MENACE	For a perfectly lovely-looking pet that wreaks havoc
DENVER	You like both the city and the singer
DEPP	For a Johnny-come-lately
DEPUTY	The guard dogs
DEPUTY DAWG	The cartoon detective from the 1960s
DERBY	A pet from Kentucky
DESDEMONA	Will live longer if not paired with Othello
DESI	For a Lucy fan
DESIGNER	Your pet makes plans in advance
DESILU	For a Lucy and Desi fan
DESIRE	Strange for a name
DESIREE	Welsh corgis . . . lively and affectionate
DESMI	Another friend from high school
DESMOND TOO TOO	So much more clever than Desmond the 'III'
DESMOND	Scottish terriers . . . lively, independent, and devoted to the family
DESOTO	For a pet soon to be obsolete
DESPERADO	You miss the good ol' cowboy movies
DESTIMONA	Lilac point Himalayans, Blue-cream points

DETOUR	For the puppy that never comes home in time
DEVINA	A divine Italian pet
DEVON	English setters, English springer spaniels, English bulldogs, etc.
DEVONSHIRE	English cocker spaniels (or all the rest)
DI	Your pet will be betrayed
DIABLO	You have a devil
DIAMOND	You have a gem
DIAMOND JIM BRADY	A rich pet . . . or an expensive one
DIAMONDS	Golden Persians, fish
DIANA	Your pet may receive somewhere in the neighborhood of $26M
DICK	See Dick, see Dick run . . . pair with Jane
DICK TRACY	Bloodhounds, coonhounds
DICKENS	For a pet that likes to creep up on you and scare the dickens out of you
DICKY	Birds
DIEGO	Don Diego, remember Zorro?
DIET	A Weight Watcher's pet
DIETER	Your pet is a finicky eater
DIETRICH	Marlene
DIJON	You love mustard
DILETTANTE	Your pet is a dabbler in or lover of the arts
DILLINGER	Any of the guard dogs or for a Cockatiel
DILLON	For a Thomas
DILLY	For a real winner . . . but what a cute name
DIMPLES	Any pet with spots, or a snake
DINA	My cousin, who changed her name from Florence . . . can't say that I blame her
DINAH	For a pet that will 'see the USA in a Chevrolet'
DINAH MO	You have a very energetic mouse

DINGER	A pet that keeps bumping into things
DINO	Fred Flintstone's pet
DION	Head of The Belmonts
DIPLOMAT	Your pet won't take sides
DIPSEY DOODLE	Your pet turns itself inside out for you
DIRK	This is a name that is very masculine, and would seem to be appropriate for any macho pet
DIRTY HARRY	A pet that takes the law into its own hands
DISCO	A '70s pet
DISCOVERY	For a pet constantly digging in the yard
DISNEY	Your pet has good family values
DISRAELI	A politician's pet
DITA	Another friend of my mother's
DITTO	Parrots
DIVINE	Remember Andy Divine?
DIXIE	Southern belles
DIXIE CUP	Any of the mini breeds
DIZZY	Either you play the trumpet or you have a gerbil with its own wheel
DJ	A radio listener's pet
DOC	A nurse's pet
DODGER	Your pet always runs away when you try to get it
DOLAN	Your pet's very good with money
DOLBY	Your dog seems to bark in surround sound
DOLLAR BILL	For a hawk or a material boy
DOLLY	For a sweet, big-busted pet
DOLORES	I'm not sure which way my son spelled Dolores or Delores . . . either way, it's a good song
DOM	Dominic's nickname
DOM PERIGNON	For a pet with a taste for the finer things in life

DOMANI	Italian greyhounds who put things off till tomorrow
DOMINGO	Spanish mastiffs who put things off till Sunday
DOMINIC	Italian hounds
DOMINIQUE	French bulldogs
DOMINO	Dalmatians
DON CORLEONE	You liked *The Godfather*
DON DIEGO	You liked *Zorro*
DON JUAN	Unneutered pets
DON QUIXOTE	Very confused pets
DONAHUE	You like Phil
DONALD	For a bridge-playing person in real estate . . . or . . . for a duck
DONATELLO	European shorthair black silver mackerel tabbies
DONNA	Best dancer, class of '65, Mamaroneck high school
DONOVAN	For a mellow, yellow pet
DONUT	For a round, jolly pet
DOODLE	For a slow-paced pet
DOOGIE	A pet that aspires to medical school at a young age
DOOLEY	Your pet hangs down his head
DOOLITTLE	You have a lazy pet
DOONEY	Burke's brother
DOORMAN	A concierge's pet
DORA	The name of an adorable dog my friend Mary brought back with her from India
DOREEN	Irish water spaniels
DORIA	*Andrea Doria*
DORIAN	For a gray pet
DORIAN GRAY	For a gray pet that will get younger
DORIS	See Horace
DORKIS	Goofy pets
DOROTHY	For anyone moving from Kansas

DORSET	A wonderful town in Vermont
DOSTOYEVSKY	Another one for any of your Russian breeds
DOT	For a tiny animal
DOTTS	Leopards
DOTTY	Dalmatians
DOUBLEDAY	Your pet gets between you and your book
DOUGH BOY	It was expensive and has a very soft belly
DOUGLAS	My cousin Diana's husband in Putney, England . . . very proper . . . very English
DOW JONES	You like to follow the market
DOW WOW	Please don't name your dog this
DOWNHILL	A skier's pet
DOWNTOWN	A dude's pet
DOWRY	It was extremely expensive
DOZER	For a cat-napper
DR. LIVINGSTON	Presumably a pet
DR. NO	It just won't do anything you want it to
DR. SEUSS	For a cat in a hat
DR. STRANGELOVE	Your pet keeps nipping you
DRACULA	Bats or Dobermans
DRAGON	For a pet with a limp
DRAKE	Paul from *Perry Mason*
DRAMA	You have a melodramatic pet
DRAPER	A pet for a person that hangs curtains for a living
DRAWERS	For the pet that gets into everything
DREAMER	See Don Quixote
DREYFUSS	The dog on *Empty Nest*
DROOPY	One of the seven dwarfs
DRUMMER	Clumber spaniels, woodpeckers
DRUMMOND	For a very rich city pet

DUANE	A southern pet
DUBUFFET	A painter's pet
DUCHESS	A pet with high aspirations
DUCKIE	A character from the movie *Pretty in Pink*
DUDE	For one cool pet
DUDLEY	Wonderful name . . . it was my nieces' cocker spaniel
DUFFY	Any of the Irish breeds, goldens, labs, for cats too . . . another all-around great name
DUFY	An artist's pet
DUKE	Pugs, Boxers
DUKE OF EARL	See Dutchy . . . the first song we ever danced to
DULCINEA	Pair with Don Quixote
DUMBO	It has big ears
DUMPLING	For a chubby little thing
DUN	Pair with Bradstreet
DUNBAR	Tawny Great Danes
DUNHILL	It lights up your life
DUNLOP	A tennis player's pet
DURAN DURAN	Great name for birds
DURANTE	Parrots, parakeets
DURBAN	South African pets
DUSHANE	Border collies
DUSTIN	What Dusty does in those closets
DUSTY	Cats that go into the far recesses of the closets
DUTCH	My college boyfriend from Holland (see Arthur)
DUTCH BOY	A painter's pet
DUTCH GIRL	A cleaner's pet
DUTCHY	My high school boyfriend . . . 9th–12th grade (interruption in 11th)
DVOŘÁK	Composer

DWEEZIL	For the son of a rock and roll star
DWINDELL	Chinese shar-peis . . . as they get larger their wrinkles dwindle
DYLAN	For a pet that whines
DYNAMITE	Hyperactive pets
DYNAMO	For a pet that just never stops

E-MAIL	You found it through the bulletin board
E.T.	Pugs or any animals that call home often
EAGAN	For a Basset Griffon Vendeen . . . courageous, tenacious, and lovable
EAMES	Has good taste in chairs
EARFUL	Parrots, mynahs, macaws
EARHART	Bird with short life expectancy
EARL	See Duke of Earl
EARL GREY	You love the tea
EARLY	For a preemie
EARNEST	For a pleaser
EARTHA	You're into kits
EARTHY	Nice excuse for your mixed breed
EAST SIDE KID	A Bowery Boy
EASTER	Bunnies who work once a year
EASTON	For a blue silver patched tabby, Maine coon . . . nice, amiable temperament
EASTSIDER	You've recently moved to the West Side—and brought the cat with you

EASTWOOD	a.k.a. Dirty Harry
EASY	Already housebroken, neutered, and doesn't shed
EASY RIDER	Horses
EASY CHAIR	Where you find it every time you come home
EASY STREET	You won the lottery and now that you no longer have to work, you can have a pet
EASY WAY	For the pet that goes in and out of the trapdoor in your house
EATON	You want it to go to private school
EBENEZER	It refuses to share
EBERT	Your pet likes movies and is all thumbs
EBONY	Any of your black pets
ECCENTRIC	A Cane Nudo or Chinese crested dog (no hair except for a tuft on its head)
ECHO	Excellent choice for parrots, macaws, etc.
ECLAIR	For a cream puff of a pet
ECLIPSE	For a pet with a black-and-white face
ECOLOGY	For a pet that cares about the environment
ECRU	Cream mackerel tabby, seal lynx shorthair, cocker spaniel, etc.
ECSTASY	Intimidating for the people in your life
EDDIE	My love
EDEN	Garden snakes
EDEN ROC	Another Miami memory
EDGAR	Will make people smile, unless you insist it's after Poe
EDGE	For a highly neurotic pet
EDISON	For a con man
EDITH	Whining voice . . . pair with Archie
EDITH WHARTON	Strong, female, American born

EDMUND	Old English sheepdogs, bulldogs, etc.
EDNA	My friend Cindy's cat. Great cat name
EDO	Japanese bobtails, Japanese spitz
EDSEL	It will soon go out of style
EDWARD	Your pedigree will fall in love with a divorced commoner
EDWARDS	You bought a lot of goldfish at once, but can't tell them apart
EDWEENA	Born old and female
EDWIN	Born old and male
EENY MEENY	Good for collections of small things . . . the others can be called Teeny Weeny, Itsy Bitsy, Miney, and Mo
EEYORE	Resembles a donkey . . . think Winnie the Pooh and Piglet
EFREM	Nostalgia for *77 Sunset Strip* and *The F.B.I.*
EGAD	You've never gotten over what it looks like
EGAN	For an Irish setter . . . energetic and full of feeling
EGBERT	May make people smile, but at your pet's expense
EGG CREAM	My absolutely favorite soda-fountain drink
EGG ROLL	Chinese shar-peis, Chow Chows, pugs
EGGHEAD	Don't do it
EGGNOG	A Christmas pet
EGO	You fell in love because it looked exactly like you
EGYPT	Egyptian maus, sphynx or other particularly exotic animals
EIDERDOWN	Angoras, Persians, Maine coons, sheepdogs, Afghans, and, of course, ducks
EIFFEL	French poodles or French bulldogs

8½	Maybe it's the markings, maybe it's the life expectancy, or maybe it's fat and reminds you of Fellini
EINSTEIN	Any animal with long white hair, the genius part will be taken for granted
EISENHOWER	A nice pet, partial to retrieving golf balls
EKG	Hyperactive pets
EL CID	Spanish mastiffs, Chihuahuas
EL DORADO	Fish with large fins
EL GRECO	Spanish greyhounds
ELAM	Persians
ÉLAN	For a pet with style
ELBA	For someone from an island
ELDERBERRY	Berry's grandparent
ELDON	For a nanny pet
ELDRIDGE	For a jail bird
ELEANOR	An independent companion with large teeth
ELECTRA	Avenging pets. Guard dogs
ELECTRIC	Luminous fish
ELEKTRA	Most becoming in the mourning
ELF	For very small pets
ELIJAH	For a pet that drinks from your cup, only you can never catch him at it
ELISHA	A pet that particularly likes a walk with the leash
ELIZABETH	English pets, whose offspring are trouble
ELKE	Swedish elkhounds
ELLEN	Not quite Helen . . . French bulldogs
ELLERY	For a queen
ELLIE	My old neighbor
ELLINGTON	A Duke's pet
ELLIOT	Makes the pet sound smart
ELIOT NESS	Guard dogs
ELLIPSIS	Dalmations

ELLIS	For a pet from an island
ELLSWORTH	For a very formal pet
ELLY MAY	A Beverly Hillbilly
ELMER	The result of inbreeding
ELMER FUDD	Anything with big ears and strange speech patterns
ELMIRA	Skinny black cats
ELOISE	The Pekingese
ELOPE	Romantic pets partial to ladders
ELROY	More dignified than the last Roy you owned
ELSA	Heroine of Wagner's *Lohengrin*
ELSIE	Either you have a cow, or it reminds you of one
ELSINORE	Great Danes
ELTON	It sounds like you know each other
ELTON JOHN	It sounds like you wish you knew each other
ELVIRA	Unsuccessful samor in Mozart's *Don Giovanni*
ELVIS	Think about it. It could be great
ELWOOD	Tall and gawky
EMAR	My friend Edgar's outdoor tabby
EMBER	Black or red pets
EMELLE	M.L. spelled out
EMERALD	You have a jewel
EMERSON	For a radio buff
EMERY	For someone that gets board easily (I hope you get that)
EMIL	For a pet from the South Pacific (I hope you got THAT)
EMILIO	Your pet has a lot of brothers
EMILY	Dickinson fans
EMIR	Oriental shorthairs
EMMA	Great name

EMMANUELLE	For an X-rated pet
EMMAUS	Pet birds
EMMERY	Has a purring quality . . . contented cats
EMMETT	A clown's pet
EMMY	A soap star's pet
EMPEROR	Tibetan terriers, Lhasa Apsos, Russian blues
EMPIRE	Either you have a very large, very high-waisted pet, or it doesn't hesitate to strike back
EMPRESS	You named your first pet Princess, but now you've grown
EMU	Bird who's lost the art of flying
ENAMEL	Turtles
ENCHILADA	Chihuahua, Mexican hairless
ENCODER	A pet with a spotted coat
ENCORE	For a brood mare
ENCYCLOPEDIA BROWN	Bloodhounds
ENERGY	Any of the terriers, hunting dogs, spooked cats
EN GARDE	Attack or guard dogs
ENGINEER	Bees, ants, pets who do things you don't quite understand
ENGLEBERT	Best when paired with a Humperdinck
ENGLISH	Yorkshire terriers, Norwich terriers, King Charles spaniels, etc.
ENGLISH CHANNEL	Your fish tank
ENGLISH MUFFIN	Any of the English breeds that are particularly endearing . . . bulldogs?
ENNUI	Lethargic pets
ENOCH	For the pet you thought had disappeared
ENOIVE	Rabbits, hamsters, gerbils
ENOUGH	For the runt of the last litter

ENVELOPE	Pet turtles
ENRIGHT	*McMillan and Wife* police officer
ENZO	You always wanted to own an Italian restaurant
ENZYME	Pets with delicate stomachs
EOS	Early risers
EPHROM	Male and funny
EPHRON	Female and funny
EPIC	A large, heroic pet
EPICENTER	A pet who demands a lot of attention
EPICURUS	Loves you for pleasure
EPILOGUE	The last of the litter
EPITOME	A pet you plan to show and win with
EPONINE	For *Les Mis* fans
EPOXY	You have a fiercely loyal pet
EPSTEIN-BARR	You have a very lethargic pet
EQUALIZER	Dobermans, Alsatians, Rottweilers, etc.
EQUINOX	An inn in Vermont
EQUUS	Pet horses
ERASMUS	The famous Brooklyn high school
ERATO	Basenjis
ERDMAN	Sounds a little like 'nerdman' . . . so, for a funny-looking pet that seems to need glasses
EREBUS	Pets with dark coats
ERGO	Any offspring of your male and female pets
ERIC	Red Abyssinians, red Devon rex, red setters, or Norwegian elkhounds
ERICA	Pets with a fear of flying
ERIN	Irish pets
ERMA	For a deuce of any kind
ERNEST	Outdoor, macho, Hemingwayesque
ERNESTO	Spanish, outdoor, macho, Hemingwayesque

ERNIE	*My Three Sons* . . . one of your three pets . . . or . . . pair with Bert if you only have two
ERNST	Miss Ernst was my grammar school gym teacher
EROS	Love birds
ERRATA	You'll regret this one
ERROL	Dark, adventurous, leading man type
ERSATZ	Mixed breeds
ERTÉ	An artist's pet
ERWIN	American foxhounds, beagles, cairn terriers, cocker spaniels, or dachshunds
ERWITT	A photogenic dog (photographer Eliot Erwitt)
ESAU	When your pet is a fable
ESCROW	The pet you've bought for protection
ESDRAS	Two books of the Old Testament
ESKIMO	Alaskan Malamutes, Eskimo dogs
ESMERELDA	Wonderful cat name, any breed
ESP	The pet that comes before you call
ESPADRILLE	A summer pet
ESPRESSO	Brown Burmese, Havana browns, Italian pointers
ESQUIRE	Wears a monocle
ESSAY	A pet who makes a statement
ESSIE	Soft-coated Wheaton terriers . . . originally from Ireland . . . courageous and active
ESTE	Means 'this' in Spanish . . . useful for gender problems
ESTEE	A pet with eyeliner markings
ESTELLE	A throwback to the '50s
ESTHER	A throwback to the Bible
ET TU?	A pet you shouldn't trust
ETCETERA	Insect collections or mutts
ETCH-A-SKETCH	Cats who claw the furniture

EVERT	Baseline fish with two-handed backstroke
EVIAN	Fresh fish . . . or a pet that won't drink from the toilet bowl
EVITA	Strong female songbirds
EWING	Great Danes, Irish wolfhounds, borzois, Scottish deerhounds
EX	Reminds you of . . .
EXAMINER	Particularly curious cats
EXCALIBUR	Snakes
EXCAVATOR	DIG, DIG,DIG
EXCESS	Breeding rabbits
EXEC	Trained to carry a briefcase
EXIT	Manx, Japanese bobtails, malamutes, Siberian huskies, etc. . . . anything with a stumped tail
EXPECTOR	Waits to greet your guests
EXPLORER	Pets who periodically disappear
EXPORT	French poodles, English spaniels, Japanese bobtails, etc.
EXPRESS	Greyhounds
EXPRESSO	Italian Greyhounds
EXPRESSWAY	For a pet that can't relax
EYEFUL	Pugs, King Charles spaniels, Cocker spaniels, anything with big eyes
EYEWITNESS	Seeing Eye dogs
EZEKIEL	A prophetic animal
EZRA	Poetic, long white beard, later may have to be institutionalized
EZRA POUND	You got him from the ASPCA

F. SCOTT	What a fabulous name for a pet
FABERGÉ	Your pet can lay eggs
FABIAN	For a songbird, with an occasional foray into movies
FABRIZIO	Italian hounds . . . strong and muscular, vivacious, hunters
FACE	For that absolutely gorgeous pet
FACT FINDER	An insurance adjuster's pet
FADDIS	Westphalian bassets . . . combative, intelligent and friendly
FADIMA	Blue Tonkinese
FAGAN	For shady characters
FAHRENHEIT	Pair with Centigrade
FAIR LADY	Lilac point Himalayans, rabbits
FAIRBANKS	Alaskan malamutes, Iceland dogs, Eskimo dogs
FAIRCHILD	English springer spaniels
FAIRFAX	An apartment building in NYC that used to be the FBI building

FAISAL	A king . . . a King Charles spaniel is of mixed ancestry, so it might work . . . good for any strong-willed pet
FAITH	For someone that believes they've found a swan
FAITHFUL	For the swan you've found. They mate for life
FA LA	For a Christmas pet . . . la la la, la la la
FALCHI	You like handbags
FALCON	Parakeets, starlings, mynahs
FALINE	A character from *Bambi*
FAMOUS AMOS	A chocolate-colored pet
FANDANGO	Trip the light fandango. Are those the right words to the song? And, what does it mean?
FANG	Phyllis Diller's husband
FANISHIA	Blue Abyssinians
FANNIE	Your pet has a broad backside
FANNY FARMER	Your pet got its broad backside eating chocolates
FANTASIA	When you can't believe that you've given in and actually gotten a pet
FANTASTIC	When Fantasia has worked out and you get a second one
FANTOM	What you wish Fantasia was if it doesn't work out
FANTUM	Same, different spelling
FANZINE	A pet that's a fan of housebreaking on magazines rather than newspapers
FARCUS	German wirehaired pointers, basset hounds, Maine coons
FARFEL	Whippets
FARFULL	Fat pets
FARKAS	Welsh corgis, scottish terriers, turtles
FARLEY	Shorthaired Saint Bernards, collies, sheepdogs
FARMER BROWN	Border collies, Shetland sheepdogs

FARNSWORTH	A character in *Heaven Can Wait* . . . I love that movie
FARNUM	Old English sheepdogs, cockatoos, snakes
FAROUK	Another king . . . King Charles spaniels
FARQUHAR	German shorthaired pointers . . . hunters, lean, exuberant, cheerful and friendly with children
FARRAH	For an Afghan . . . great hair
FARRER	Smooth fox terriers
FARRIS	Westphalian bassets
FAST FORWARD	Another one for the hyperactive type
FAT CAT	Just that
FATAL ATTRACTION	For a pet that you can't resist, who will eventually be your undoing
FATHER MULCAHY	Another of the *M*A*S*H* characters
FATIMA	Egyptian maus, salukis
FALKLAND	For a pet from an island
FAULKNER	English bulldogs
FAUNA	Pair with Flora
FAUST	English foxhounds
FAUZI	Pharaoh hounds
FAWN	Fawn Abyssinians
FAX	For a very busy pet
FAY	For a non-pedigree longhair
FAY WRAY	It's married to a gorilla
FEARLESS	It IS the gorilla married to Fay Wray
FEATHER	I went to high school with a girl named Feather
FEATHERS	Birds
FEATHERWEIGHT	Light pets
FEBRUARY	Your pet was born in February
FEDERICO	For a Fellini fan
FEE FEE	French bulldogs . . . good name
FEEDBACK	Parrots, macaws, mynahs

FEENEY	Shirleys
FEETS	For pets able to leap tall buildings in a single bound with multicolored paws
FEIFFER	Jules or Michelle fans
FELDER	You've just gotten divorced
FELICE	Happy, in Spanish
FELICIA	For a happy Cane Nudo
FELICIANO	A pet into lighting fires
FELICITY	A very happy pet
FELIX	The cat, the wonderful, wonderful cat . . . or . . . pair with Oscar
FELLAH	For a 'most happy'
FELLER	Male Labrador retrievers
FELLINI	Italian pointers . . . thoughtful, docile, loyal, not excessively cheerful
FEMME FATALE	You have a breeding pet
FENDI	You're into labels
FENIMORE	A street in Mamaroneck, New York
FENWAY	A stadium in Boston
FENWICK	A street in Waban, Massachusetts
FERDINAND	The Bull . . . possibly, also Isabella's husband
FERGI	A red Royal Standard
FERGUS	Golden retrievers, Scottish terriers
FERGUSON	Another wonderful pet name
FERNANDO	Your cat likes to 'hide away'
FERRAGAMO	Italian pointers
FERRARI	Italian greyhounds
FERRIS	Gerbils . . . round and round and round and round
FESTER	I would use this for a slightly distasteful pet
FETA	Greek hounds
FETCHIT	You have a comedian on your hands
FIAT	European shorthair cream-shaded cameo tabbies
FIBBER MCGEE	And Molly

FIDDLER	A roofer's pet
FIDDLESTICKS	Your pet is skinny
FIDEL	Your pet is a dictator
FIDO	Well, finally, a name that's really a name!
FIELD MARSHAL	Deutsche dogges
FIELDER	Your pet likes to chase balls
FIGARO	An opera lover's pet
FIEVEL	Your pet will be going west
FIGI	Singapore
FIJIT	Hyperactives
FILBERT	For a nut
FILENE	A pet that will live in the basement
FILIBUSTER	Parrots, mynah birds
FILLIPA	Swedish shepherds . . . courageous and independent
FILO DOUGH	For a Greek hound that enjoys a good pastry now and then
FILOFAX	A very organized person's pet
FINANCE	An accountant's pet
FINCHLEY	My father's sister Shirley lives in Finchley, England
FINDLAY	A gallery
FINDLEY	A mere name
FINGERPRINT	A policeman's dog
FINKE	Finnish hounds
FINNEUS	Scottish terriers
FINNIAN	*Finnian's Rainbow* . . . the first play I was ever in
FINOLA	Finnish spitz
FIONA	Any English pet with a bent towards snobbish behavior
FIORELLO	You fly to LaGuardia a lot
FIRE-EATER	Pit bulls, Dobermans
FIREWATER	For a cat that keeps trying to get into the fish tank

FIREWORKS	For the cat that succeeds in getting into the fish tank
FIROOZ	Egyptian maus, pharaoh dogs
FIRST LADY	A female pet for a household of boys
FIRSTLUFF	You finally got one you love
FISH	Portuguese water dogs, Irish water dogs
FITCHLY	Great Pyrenees . . . very big, hardworking, and affectionate
FITZGERALD	Any of the Irish breeds
FITZI	Fitzpatrick and Fitzgerald's nickname
FITZPATRICK	Fitzi's full name
FLACK	You either love Roberta or your pet talks back
FLAME	Any of the red breeds
FLAN	A dessert lover's pet
FLAPJACK	A pancake lover's pet
FLASH	For a very fast pet
FLASH DANCE	For a pet so fast that it looks like dancing
FLASH GORDON	Those were the days
FLATFOOT	Another policeman's pet
FLAUBERT	French novelist . . . *Madame Bovary*
FLEETWOOD	A chauffeur's pet
FLEISCHMANN	You can't believe it's not pedigree
FLETCH	A bumbling detective
FLETCHER	A mystery writer's pet
FLINTSTONE	If you really loved them, go for it
FLIP	Your pet does somersaults
FLIPPER	Fish
FLOPPER	Your pet doesn't quite execute the full somersault
FLORA	Turtles, garden snakes, frogs . . . green things
FLORENCE	A wonderful city in Italy . . . see Dina
FLORIDA	You won't be retiring soon enough
FLORIE	For a Siamese
FLORIS	Shorthaired Scottish folds

FLOSSIE	A dentist's pet
FLOSSY	Same
FLOUR	A cook's pet
FLOWER	A gardener's pet
FLOYD	A boxer's pet
FLYING SORCERER	Birds
FM	A DJ's pet
FODOR	Either for the guide or the guide dog
FODORA	For a Himalayan longhaired
FOGEL	Irish wolfhounds
FOGGY	Your pet has a poor sense of direction
FOLDER	You have a soft spot for Manila
FOLLY	You know, in your heart, it's going to be a mistake
FOLY	Skye terriers
FONDUE	Another cheesy name
FONTEYN	West Highland white terriers
FOO FOO	Samoyeds . . . they just look foo foo, all puffy, fluffy, and white
FOOSHA	Oriental shorthairs
FOOTPRINT	Newfoundlands. Now that's a footprint
FORBES	An intelligent pet
FORD	A pet from Harrison
FOREMAN	Staffordshire bull terriers . . . combative but steady
FOREPLAY	For a dog that likes to tease before biting
FORESIGHT	A dog that doesn't use foreplay
FOREST	Black Forest hounds . . . the Czechoslovakian national hound . . . independent with a good sense of direction
FORMAGGIO	An Italian animal partial to hard, grating cheeses
FORSYTH	For a pet that has foresight, but also a lisp
FORT APACHE	It came from the Bronx

FORTESQUE	Although a great name for any male, I like it for the Scottish terrier
FORTUNE	Any pet that cost over $500
FOSDICK	Maine coons
FOSSE	A dancer's pet
FOSTER	Your pet wears sunglasses, and your name is Grant
FOTO	A photographer's pet
FOUAD	Pharaoh hounds . . . loyal and very playful
FOULARD	A tie maven's pet
FOUNTAINBLEU	For someone who used to travel to Miami in the '60s
FOURTH OF JULY	A pet born on the 4th of July
FOUZI	Egyptian maus, salukis
FOXIE	American fox terriers
FRACK	Pair with Frick
FRANCHESCA	Female Spanish greyhounds . . . aristocratic and courageous
FRANCIS	Anglo-Spanish greyhounds
FRANCISCO	Male Spanish greyhounds
FRANCO	For a Spanish mastiff dictator
FRANK	American foxhounds
FRANKFURTER	A judgmental dachshund
FRANKIE	His nickname
FRANKLIN	My cousin in California . . . he used to have a dog named Rover!
FRANKO	Spinone Italianos . . . although they are gentle and good-natured
FRANZ	For someone who is on the list
FRANZETTI	My dear high school friend. We used to have wonderful parties in her basement
FRASIER	A psychiatrist's pet
FRAU ZEITZ	My German teacher

FRAÜLEIN	My German teacher . . . we called her Frau, but we knew that she was really a Fraülein
FRAZER	Wirehaired dachshunds
FRECKLES	Dalmatians
FRED	Great name
FREDDIE	I love this name
FREDDY	No matter how you spell it
FREDERIC	Miniature schnauzers, Lhasa Apsos, malamutes
FREDERICK	For someone who dresses from Hollywood
FREEDOM	Border collies or Bosnian hounds
FREELANCE	A pet that has more than one owner
FREEWAY	The dog from the series *Hart to Hart*
FRENCH FRY	French spaniels
FRENCH TOAST	French pointers, poodles, minis, French bulldogs
FRESH	Your pet is 'cool'
FRET	A guitarist's pet
FREUD	Your pet understands your deepest thoughts
FRIAR TUCK	It will live with you in a forest
FRICK	A museum in New York
FRIDAY	My gal
FRIEDA	For a German shorthair from the Lower East Side
FRIEND HARE	A character from *Bambi*
FRISBEE	For a dog you have to catch
FRISKIE	Definitely for one of the terriers or schnauzers
FRISKY	Same
FRITZ	Another one of my favorite names
FRITZI	Also
FRIVULUS	You just wanted to, that's why
FRIZZY	Pulis . . . they have those long curly locks that reach the ground

FROMAGE	A French animal partial to soft, runny cheeses
FROMM	An analyst's pet
FROSTIE	Siberian huskies
FROSTING	Your pet is not satisfied with its hair color
FROSTY	Iceland dogs, snowmen
FRUMPSON	For the son of a frump
FU MANCHU	For any of your Chinese breeds . . . Lhasa Apsos, Shih Tzus, Chow Chows, shar-peis, etc.
FUCHSIA	A colorful pet
FUCILLI	Another one for pulis . . . long, curly hair
FUDGE	A chocoholic's pet
FUGITIVE	The pet that keeps running away
FULLER BRUSH MAN	Your pet goes from house to house
FUNK	A depressed pet
FUNKY	A happy pet
FUNNY FACE	For Fred Astaire and Audrey Hepburn fans
FURROUK	A furry king
FUTURE SHOCK	For a pet that will grow far bigger than you anticipated
FUZZY	For a pet with memory loss
FUZZY WUZZY	What they said about Fuzzy

G-STRING	French poodles, French bulldogs
G.I. JOE	Definitely for boxers, or bulldogs, or wirehaired dachshunds
GABBI	One of those adorable names that would be good for any cute animal
GABBY HAYES	Roy Rogers sidekick
GABE	Always reminds me of *Welcome Back, Kotter*
GABLE	You like Clark
GABOR	You have a femme fatale
GABRIEL	Your pet blows a horn
GABRIELLE	For a more formal cute animal
GAEL	Frogs, turtles, lizards
GAIETY	For an absolutely, positively, constantly happy pet
GAINESFORT	For a slower-moving animal, like an English mastiff
GAINSBOROUGH	Your pet knows good art when it sees it
GAL FRIDAY	You bring it to the office with you
GALATEA	Very regal . . . for a pet with extreme poise and great posture

GALAXY	For a pet that's got his head in the clouds
GALBRAITH	An economical pet
GALILEO	You have a stargazer
GALLANT	A polite pet
GALLOP	Horses
GALLUP	Horses that jump polls
GAMBLER	Either your pet does tightrope tricks or it will travel to Vegas a lot
GAMEBOY	Your home is addicted to the game
GANNETT	Your pet only uses local papers
GARBO	It 'vants to be alone'
GARCIA	Spanish mastiffs
GARÇON	A waiter's pet
GARDENER	Your pet is constantly digging up the yard
GARDENIA	For a white Persian or a Vincent
GARFIELD	If you do it, people will marvel at your lack of originality
GARFUNKEL	Songbirds
GARIBALDI	Italian patriot
GARLAND	Judy, Judy, Judy
GARLIC	Your pet has bad breath
GARLIK	It will use the pills
GARNET	Red Abyssinians, red setters, red poodles
GARP	For a pet that thinks the world goes according to it
GARRETT	For a Prairie Home companion
GARRISON	A pet from Lake Wobegon
GARRON	A $250 per haircut hairdresser in NY (at this writing)
GARROWAY	For a faithful *Today Show* fan
GARTH	For a pet that will eventually live on a brook
GARVEY	I know a realtor by this name
GARY	A pet from Indiana

GASSMAN	A Con Ed man's pet
GATEWAY	A bridge inspector's pet
GATSBY	A rich, loose pet
GATWAY	Blue-cream smoke Cornish rexes
GATWICK	You travel to England frequently
GAUDY	For a very ostentatious pet
GAUGUIN	Artist
GAZA	For a patrol dog
GAZA STRIPPER	For a Cane Nudo . . . (no hair, just a tuft on its head)
GAZELLA	Greyhounds, nice and fast
GAZPACHO	For a Heinz 57 variety
GEDRICK	Sounds like a hairstylist
GEEWIZ	For your very innocent, naive pet
GEISHA	Japanese bobtails, Japanese spitzes
GEM	For a pearl of a pet
GEMINI	It was born in June
GEMMA	A gemologist's pet
GENERAL	Boxers, bulldogs, or other authoritative types
GENESIS	A teenager's pet
GENEVA	Swiss hounds
GENIUS	Either a very smart or a very dumb pet
GENOA	Italian pointers, Italian Greyhounds etc.
GENTLE BEN	CBS TV show . . . 1967–69
GEOFFREY	For a ballet aficionado
GEORGE	Boy
GEORGETOWN	A politician's pet
GEORGETTE	Ted's wife on *The Mary Tyler Moore Show*
GEORGIA	Georgia on your mind
GEORGIA BROWN	A sweet pet
GEORGINA	For a feisty Georgia
GEORGIO	For a very suave Spinone Italiano (dog)

GERALD	For a not-so-suave American blue tick coonhound
GERALDINE	For a female, not-so-suave American blue tick coonhound
GERALDO	A feisty pet
GERANIUM	Pets with big, sweet faces
GERARD	English mastiffs
GERARDO	Spanish mastiffs
GERBER	Your pet has a baby face
GERBER BABY	Your pet is going to be spoon-fed
GERMAINE	For a pet that makes a difference
GERONIMO	Your pet has no boundaries
GERRI	German spaniels
GERSHWIN	For a cat that walks the piano keys
GERT	For
GERTIE	a
GERTRUDE	cat
GESTALT	Your pet gets the whole picture
GET SMART	For a Maxwell
GETTYSBURG	Your pet knows its address
GHIDRAH	The three-headed monster
GHOST	For an all white pet, and Mrs. Muir
GHOSTBUSTER	For a bigger and meaner pet than Ghost
GIACOMETTI	Artist
GIANNI	Continental spaniels, minis
GIBSON	Bedlington terriers
GIBSON GIRL	Fat chance
GIDEON	A pet with a horn
GIDGET	Sandra Dee . . . the Big Cahuna . . . family values
GIFFORD	A pet that follows football . . . pair with Kathy Lee
GIGGLES	It just looks like it's laughing all the time
GIGI	French bulldogs
GILBERT	Chow Chows

GILBERT GRAPE	Chow Chows that like grapes
GILDA	For a wonderful, funny pet
GILES	For a butler, or you have a penguin
GILL	Fish
GILLESPIE	Dizzy pets
GILLETTE	For a sharp guy
GILLI	Bedlington terriers . . . look like sheep and like to catch rats
GILLIGAN	For a pet you'd like to send to an island
GILLIS	Dobie . . . 1962
GILLYFLOWER	Such a cute name . . . a wiggly, happy silky terrier
GILMORE	Cocker spaniels or chocolate tortie Burmese
GILROY	Cairn terriers . . . lively, cheerful and lovable . . . Toto from *The Wizard of Oz*
GIMBEL'S	Will not live as long as Macy's
GIMLET	Saint Bernards
GINGER	There are an amazing number of dogs named Ginger
GINGER ROGERS	More original than just plain Ginger
GINGERBREAD	An alternative to Ginger
GINO	For a Bolognese
GIORDANO	Italian greyhounds
GIORGIO	A pet from Beverly Hills
GIOVANNA	A female pet recently over from Italy
GIOVANNI	A male pet recently over from Italy
GIRL SCOUT	For a real goody two shoes
GISH	Lillian and Dorothy
GIUSEPPE	See Pedro . . . his partner, also with a Mercedes
GIVENCHY	For a very fancy, well-dressed pet
GIZMO	An inventor's pet
GLADIOLA	For a very feminine, flowery pet

GLADYS	What a name. Actually, it was my grandmother's name and she reminded me of a bulldog (sorry Nana)
GLAMOR PUSS	That is just so cute
GLEE	For a particularly happy pet
GLEN	For a tall, dark, male outdoor pet
GLENDA	For a tall, dark, female outdoor pet
GLENLIVET	A drinker's pet
GLICK	For one of the smaller animals . . . like hamsters, turtles, fish, etc.
GLOO POT	Horses . . . just kidding
GLORIA	American wirehair calicos
GLORY	Red, white, and blue American short-hairs
GLOVER	For a baseball catcher
GNASHER	Pair with Wolf from *Wuthering Heights* . . . or . . . a pet with huge teeth
GNOCCHI	You love potatoes
GOALIE	Jack Russells . . . they keep going after that ball
GOBLET	Your pet will eat from a silver bowl and drink from a silver cup
GOBO	A character from *Bambi*
GODDARD	You love to clean silver
GODFATHER	Rottweilers, Great Danes, mastiffs
GODFREY	My Man
GODFRIED	English foxhounds
GODIVA	Another good name for Afghans
GODZILLA	For a very menacing pet
GOITER	Ooh, I don't like it
GOLD DIGGER	A weak male golden retriever
GOLD DUST	You haven't quite hit pay dirt
GOLD RUSH	A golden retriever moving to California
GOLDA	A strong female golden retriever
GOLDEN BOY	Golden retriever
GOLDEN GIRL	Golden retriever

GOLDFINGER	Golden retriever
GOLDIE	Golden retriever
GOLDILOCKS	Golden retriever (or pulis)
GOLDWATER	A republican golden retriever . . . or . . . one that's not quite housebroken
GOLIATH	Irish wolfhounds, borzois, deerhounds . . . any pet that can put its paws on your shoulders when it jumps up to greet you
GOMER	A pet that leaves a pile
GOMEZ	A suave character
GONPOTEE	The housebreaking has just proven impossible
GONZALEZ	Mexican hairless dogs
GONZO	You're into Muppets . . . or . . . your pet is slightly nutty
GOOBER	You love going to the movies . . . Pair with Raisinette
GOOD AND PLENTY	Dalmatians . . . or . . . big animals, like Saint Bernards
GOOD KING WENCESLAS	You have a jolly, fat pet
GOODSPEED	A fast pet
GOODWILL	A pet from the ASPCA
GOOFY	Disney's 'goofy' dog
GOOSEBERRY	Small pets
GOOSEBUMP	Even smaller pets
GOOSEBUMPS	Your pet gets scared easily
GOPHER	For a *Love Boat* fan
GORBACHEV	A formal Russian wolfhound
GORBIE	An informal Russian wolfhound
GORDIE HOWE	You love hockey
GORDIMER	For an English/German mix
GORDON	You're a gin lover
GORDY	*Stand By Me*

**GORGEOUS
GEORGE**   George Wagner, the wrestler . . . good for blonde pets

GORKY   It likes the park

GOSSETT   Tall, lean muscular pets with fierce eyes

GOTFRIED   German shepherds, German shorthaired pointers

GOTHAM   Another choice for a silver cleaning fanatic or a Batman fan

GOUDA   Contains more fat than Edam

GOURMET   Your pet won't touch dry food

GOVERNOR   It will eventually run for president

GOYA   You didn't realize it was so full of beans

GRABLE   You bought it because of its legs

GRACE   For a religious pet

GRACIE   You loved Burns and Allen

GRACIELLA   Italian pointers . . . although they tend not to be too cheerful

GRADUATE   A pet that will have to go through obedience training more than once

GRADY   A scruffy pet

GRAF   A tennis aficionado's pet

GRAFFITI   Your pet likes to mark his territory

GRAHAM   For a cracker or a dog

GRAINGER   American foxhounds

**GRAND
MARNIER**   An after dinner pet

GRAND PRIX   A race car driver's pet

GRAND SLAM   A tennis player's pet

GRANDE DAME   Wonderful for Saint Bernards, borzois, Newfoundlands, etc.

**GRANDMA
MOSES**   Chinese shar-peis (wrinkles)

GRANGER   I like this name. It's strong and seems excellent for a confident pet

GRANITE   You got one that won't budge

GRANNIE	Another good one for the shar-pei
GRANOLA	You have a lumpy pet
GRANT	Another Confederate pet
GRAPHIC	A pet that uses its paws when communicating
GRAVLAX	Fish or cats
GRAY	Silver tabby Persians . . . (they look gray)
GRAZIELLA	Maltese, Italian pointers
GRAZIE	A very thankful pet
GREAT GATSBY	Harlequin Great Danes
GRECO	Spanish water dogs
GREELEY	Horace
GREEN BERET	Bulldogs, boxers, Rottweilers, or pit bulls . . . good in the protection area
GREENSTREET	Sydney . . . good for a fat pet
GREENWICH	A pet from Connecticut
GREER	A pet for a feminist
GREGORY	Woodpeckers
GREMLIN	Pugs or King Charles spaniels
GRETA	You like Garbo
GRETCHEN	Sounds very reliable
GRETEL	Hansel's pair . . . and my friend Joan's mother
GREY	Silver spotted British shorthairs (it looks grey)
GREYSTOKE	Monkeys
GRIFFEN	Parakeets
GRIFFIN	Pair with Sabine . . . lovebirds
GRIMALDI	A pet from Monaco
GRIMES	Tennessee treeing brindles
GRIMM	You're either depressed or you like fairy tales
GRINGO	For a non-Mexican pet
GRISELDA	Great cat name

GRISWALD	Royal Standards
GRIZZARD	Cross between a gizzard and a lizard
GRODY	A tough little Scottish terrier
GROMYKO	Russian wolfhounds, Russian blues, borzois
GROUCHO	Either you are a grouch or you like the Marx Brothers
GROVER	Your pet is from Cleveland
GSTAAD	A skier's pet
GUARDIAN	Rottweilers, pit bulls, Dobermans
GUCCI	Triple with Fendi and Mark Cross
GUESS	A pet of mixed parentage
GUGGENHEIM	Your pet appreciates museums
GUILLERMO	A Spanish William
GUINEVERE	That naughty queen from Camelot
GUINNESS	For an Alec or a beer lover
GULLIVER	Pets that like to travel
GUMBLE	Early morning pets
GUMBO	Pets that like soup
GUMP	For an incredibly lucky, very limited pet
GUNNAR	German shorthair pointers
GUNS	Pair with Roses
GUNSMOKE	You watched TV in the '60s
GUS	Basset hounds
GUSSIE	For American pets
GUSTAF	For French pets
GUSTAV	For German pets
GUSTAVO	For Spanish pets
GUSTO	For a pet with a flair for eating big and quick
GUSTOFF	For Swiss pets
GUTHRIE	For an Arlo
GUY	Pair with Gal
GWEN	Shorthair cream lynx point rexes
GWENDOLYN	Longhair cream silver Somalis

GWYNNE	Cockatiels
GYPSY	Multicolored, orange, white and black cats
GYPSY ROSE LEE	See Gaza Stripper

H. STERN	For a jewel of a pet, with franchises all over the world
HAAIG	Someone I had a crush on in high school
HABIBI	This is for a real sweetheart (Arabic)
HABUBAH	Another Arabic name for sweetheart
HACKETT	He will be your buddy
HADDIE	Black Forest hounds, fish, hamsters
HAILEY	Brown California spangled longhairs
HAKEEM THE DREAM	Olajuwon
HAKIM	If you're into Arabic names . . . this one means doctor
HALEVI	Yugoslavian tricolor hounds, guinea pigs
HALF PINT	Cute for small animals
HALFBACK	Cute for big animals
HALIFAX	For cold animals
HALIMA	European shorthair tortie smokes
HALLE	Dutch sheepdogs, Pomeranians
HALLEY	The comet . . . for a pet you expect to live till the age of 76

ETHAN	Partial to antique furniture
ETHAN ALLEN	Partial to antique furniture reproductions
ETHEL	Lucy's friend and neighbor
ETHER	For sleepy pets
ETHYL	Your pet's into alcohol
ETON	English bulldogs, English spaniels, etc.
ETON ALLEN	Same, but, partial to English antique furniture reproductions
ETOS	Greyhounds . . . intelligent, but often undervalued because of its reserved behavior
ETTA	Pair her with Quette
EUCLID	Pets with geometric markings
EUGENE	For a pet who is definitely not the nickname type
EUNICE	Funny-looking female
EUPHORIA	Uncaged birds
EUREKA	The pet that replaces your vacuum when it comes to cleaning up the kitchen floor
EUROPA	Bulldogs
EUSTACE	Funny-looking males
EVA	My oldest and dearest childhood friend
EVAN	I like it for a collie. After all, they can't all be Lassie
EVANS	Rogers's mate
EVE	First born female. See Adam
EVELYN	Usually your best friend's mother
EVENING SHADE	Deep gray or blue to black coloring
EVEREST	A very tall example of its species
EVERETT	For a pet that doesn't like to be cooped up . . . (C. Everett)
EVERGLADE	A pet from Florida
EVERGREEN	Turtles and frogs who live to a ripe old age

HALLIE	American wirehair brown mackerel tabbies
HALSEY	Lavender classic tabbies
HALSTON	A designer's pet
HAMILL	A journalist's or skater's pet
HAMILTON	A politician's pet
HAMISH	For a very affectionate lapdog
HAMLET	An English major's pet
HAMLISCH	You enjoy Marvin
HAMMACHER	A shopper's pet
HAMMARSKJÖLD	For a UN pet . . . mixed
HAMMERSTEIN	Pair with Oscar
HAMPDEN	American foxhounds
HAMPTON	You like Long Island
HANCOCK	Your pet has a good signature
HANDEL	Composer
HANDLEY	Monkeys
HANDSOME DAN	The Yale mascot . . . (white bulldog)
HANDY	Your pet can fix things
HANGAR	A pilot's pet
HANINA	Egyptian maus
HANK	A tough guy pet
HANKS	A Tom cat
HANNAH	A soft, motherly pet
HANNIBAL	A great warrior
HANS	For a Christian Andersen
HANTUSHA	My Lhasa Apso's (Tusha) formal name . . . it means sweetheart
HAPPINESS	Your pet has a perpetual smile on its face
HAPPY	Your pet is everything you could wish for
HAPPY TRAILS	You remember watching *The Roy Rogers Show*
HARBOR MASTER	Any of the water spaniels

HARD ROCK	You enjoy going to cafes
HARDING	A presidential pet
HARDWICKE	Pit bulls, lizards
HARDY	Pair with Laurel
HARKNESS	For a pet with large ears and great hearing
HARLEAN	Harlequin Great Danes
HARLEY	You can't get the bike, so the pet gets the name
HARLOT	Well, I don't think so
HARLOW	You have a sexy pet
HARMONY	For a pet that receives strangers well
HAROLD	My uncle . . . I have to be nice . . . especially since he saved me from being named Hazel
HARPER	You have a Bazaar pet
HARPIGNIES	Artist's pet
HARPO	Your pet is mute
HARRIMAN	For a very distinguished, diplomatic pet
HARRINGTON	Irish setters, Irish wolfhounds
HARRIS	It's a poll taker
HARRISON	You drive a Ford
HARRY	For a dirty dog (two puns in one!)
HARRY WINSTON	You want something from the store, but, like Harley, you'll have to settle for the pet
HART	Hartley's nickname
HARTLEY	Your pet would wear tassel loafers if it could
HARVARD	An Ivy Leaguer's pet
HARVEST	A pet from the Midwest
HARVEY	Rabbits
HARVEY WALLBANGER	Rabbits that drink too much
HASKELL	*Leave It to Beaver's* pal Eddie
HASLETT	Doctor in *Murder, She Wrote*

HASSAN	Horses
HASSELHOFF	For any of the water spaniels
HASTY	For a pet you chose incorrectly
HASTY PUDDING	For a funny Yorkshire terrier
HATTIE	Collies
HAVI	For the separated part of a Siamese
HAVOC	Your pet will take over your household
HAWK	Dobermans, crows
HAWKEYE	Bird dogs
HAWKINS	A pet for a Sadie
HAWORTH	Blue tick coonhounds
HAYAKAWA	Dogs that sleep all the time
HAYDN	Composer's pet
HAYES	My son Adam's middle name
HAYWORTH	The Rita that I was named for. Can you imagine?
HAZEL	What my parents tried to name me before my Uncle Harold intervened. Can you imagine?
HEALER	A doctor's pet
HEARST	You love magazines
HEART	For a pet near and dear
HEATH BAR	For a chocolate-and-toffee colored animal
HEATHCLIFF	A dark, brooding, and romantic English pet
HEATHCOTE	Old English mastiffs
HEATHER	Quiet, gentle pets
HEATHROW	A stewardess's pet
HECTOR	Spanish greyhounds
HECTOR GARCIA	Who IS Hector Garcia?
HEFNER	For the head bunny
HEIDI	For a Swiss hound
HEIFETZ	A musician's pet
HEINZ	Pets of mixed parentage

HELMSLEY	Your pet has tax problems
HELMUT	Great for a Doberman
HELOISE	Your pet likes to give hints
HEMINGWAY	You have an ernest pet
HENDERSON	A pet for a Florence
HENDRIX	A pet for a Jimi
HENLEY	Gordon setters
HENNY YOUNGMAN	A comedian's pet
HENREICH	You like the Yankees
HENRI	For a Bendel's shopper
HENRIETTA	For a female Bendel's shopper
HENRIK	For a German Bendel's shopper
HENRY	For an American Bendel's shopper
HENRY BROWN	A farmer's pet
HEPBURN	You watch *Breakfast at Tiffany's* more than once a year
HEPWORTH	Clumber spaniels, hamsters, mynahs
HER	Double with Him
HERA	Zeus's sister
HERBERT	One of the great names
HERBIE	Herbert's nickname
HERCEMER	Red Abyssinians, Pomeranians, snakes
HERCULE	For Poirot fans
HERCULES	Either a Yorkie or a Rottweiler
HERE'S JOHNNY	A late night pet
HERMALENE	Rhodesian ridgebacks
HERMAN	A hermit
HERMÈS	Your pet will wear a scarf
HERMINIE	Wonderful for a big, fat, furry cat
HERMITAGE	Russian pets
HERNANDO	A pet that knows how to hide away
HERO	You either have a Saint Bernard or you are partial to the sandwich
HERRINGBONE	For a cross between a dog and cat . . . herring for the cat and bone for the dog

HERSCHEL	What a name for a basset hound
HERSHEL	Silver spotted British shorthairs
HERSHEY	You love chocolate
HERTZ	You're always renting
HESPERUS	Evening star
HESTER	A pet found on the Lower East Side
HEYERDAHL	Thor . . . *Kon Tiki,* the first nonfiction book I read and liked
HEYWARD	For a person that calls Ward often
HEYWOOD	For a person that calls Wood often
HI	Makes it quicker to greet it
HIALIAH	Greyhounds, horses
HIAM	La . . . for a healthy pet
HICCUP	Another good one for Saint Bernards
HICKORY	A smoked pet
HIGGINS	Actually, the 7th-grade teacher that made us read *Kon Tiki*
HIGH ANXIETY	A Mel Brooks type
HIGH CLASS	A Grace Kelly type
HIGH ENERGY	A Jerry Lewis type
HIGH SOCIETY	A Bing Crosby type
HIGHNESS	Irish wolfhounds, deerhounds, borzois
HILDA	German shepherds
HILDEGARDE	Her sister
HILTON	Your pet will travel well
HIM	Double with Her
HINDRANCE	Your pet won't travel well
HINLEY	Oriental reds
HIPPOCRATES	For a healthy pet
HIROHITO	Japanese spitz
HIROSHIGE	Japanese spaniels
HIRSCHL	Cream tabby point Devon rexes
HITCHCOCK	Your pet is a mystery to you
HOAGY	Dachshunds
HOBART	Great Pyrenees
HOBSON	Irish setters

HOCKNEY	Your pet is into swimming pools
HODGE	Double with Podge
HODGES	For a pet that serves you
HOFFA	A pet that's neither here nor there
HOGAN	A scrappy, wiry mutt
HOGAN'S HERO	The owner of the scrappy, wiry mutt
HOKUSAI	Japanese bobtails
HOLDEN	A pet for a William
HOLIDAY	You bought it on vacation
HOLLING	You miss *Northern Exposure*
HOLLY	A hunter's pet
HOLLYWOOD	You have a real show dog
HOLMES	A detective's pet
HOME BOY	One of the cats in the hood
HOMER	I actually have a beautiful ragdoll (cat) named Homer . . . and we love baseball
HONEY	A favorite for golden retrievers
HONEY BUN	Any golden-color pet
HONEYCHARM	Another good name for goldens
HONEYMIST	Golden persians
HONEYSUCKLE	For a Rose
HONG-CHOO	Chinese temple dogs, Lhasa Apsos
HONUS	You're a baseball fanatic
HOODLUM	For one of those pets that has circles around its eyes
HOOLIGAN	A naughty dachshund
HOOVER	A pet that eats absolutely everything in sight
HOPKINS	English springer spaniels, boxers
HOPSACK	Akitas
HORACE	When was the last time you met a Horace?
HORATIO	Giant schnauzers
HORNE	For a pet that lets you lean (Lena) on it
HOROSCOPE	An astrologer's pet
HORTENSE	An elephant

HORTON	An elephant too
HOSMER	A Swedish shepherd
HOSS	Brother to Little Joe and Adam
HOT DIGGIDY DOG	A dachshund who can jump up and click his heels on receiving good news
HOT DOG	A dachshund
HOT FLASH	A dachshund either entering or leaving menopause
HOT FUDGE	A dachshund who's overweight
HOT LIPS	A dachshund with sex appeal
HOT ROD	A dachshund who runs fast
HOT TAMALE	A dachshund from Mexico
HOT TODDY	A dachshund who drinks
HOTFOOT	A dachshund who knows when to leave the scene fast
HOTHOUSE FLOWER	A dachshund called Orchid for short
HOTSHOT	A dachshund who throws his money around
HOUDINI	A disappearing dachshund
HOUGHTON	An Irish dachshund
HOUSTON	A Texas dachshund
HOWARD	A rich dachshund
HOWARD HUGE	An exceptionally large dachshund
HOWDY DOODY	A baby boomer's dachshund
HOWELL	A dachshund stuck on Gilligan's Island
HUBBARD	A mother dachshund
HUBBLE	A three-legged dachshund
HUBERT	Turtles, fish, frogs
HUBIE	Cream point birmans
HUCK FINN	A pet that likes to travel, preferably by raft
HUCKLEBERRY FINN	A pet that likes to travel, preferably by yacht

HUCKLEBERRY HOUND	The favorite cartoon character
HUD	For a very sexy, tough-looking, yet vulnerable, pet
HUDSON	Fish
HUEY	Your last name is Lewis
HUGH	Pugs
HUGO	I like it for a shar-pei
HUMBOLDT	Harlequin Great Danes
HUMPERDINCK	Parrots, mynahs
HUMPHREY	See Eva . . . she has a bichon named Humphrey
HUNT	For a fox
HUNTER	For any of the hunting animals
HUNTLEY	Pair with Brinkley
HURLY	Pair with Burly
HURRICANE	Your pet came from Miami
HUSSEIN	King Charles spaniels, Royal Standards
HUSSEY	The second wife that overlapped the first
HUTCH	Another high school notable
HUTCHINGS	English cocker spaniels
HUTTON	A model pet
HUXFORD	American foxhounds
HUXLEY	Scottish terriers
HYME	Yorkshire terriers
HYRAM	You've given him the job

I N X S	You have a large pet
I, CLAUDIUS	An egocentric pet who looks good in a toga
I.C.U.	Your pet likes to play peekaboo
I.D.	Paranoid pets
I.Q.	Pets who test well
IAGO	Bad character, watch out
IAN	Pet with a purpose
IBM	A pet that can honestly say "I've Been Moved"
IBSEN	It will live in a doll's house
ICARUS	A pet with an agenda
ICE CAP	For a bulldog with a hat
ICE CREAM	For the pet who hasn't yet discovered frozen yogurt
ICE CUBE	Your pet loves being in the water
ICEBERG	Samoyeds, Akitas, Iceland dogs
ICED TEA	Your pet likes to sit on the porch
ICELANDER	Your pet enjoys skidding across frozen ponds

ICEMAN	For pets who cometh when you calleth
ICHABOD	You have a crane
ID	For a pet with a conscience
IDA	English bulldogs, fish, starlings
IDDY	Iddy, biddy pets
IDRIS	Honey mink Tonkinese
IDYLL	You have a very idyllic, pastoral pet
IGGY	Dandie Dinmont terriers, cairn terriers, lizards, fish
IGLOO	Alaskan malamutes, Eskimo dogs
IGNACE	Cream Turkish vans
IGNACOUS	Scottish terriers
IGNATIUS	Giant schnauzers
IGNI	A pyromaniac's pet
IGOR	What a great name. Russian wolfhounds
IKE	You're a Republican
IKEHORN	You loved *Scruples*
IL DUCHE	Your pet loves bathing
ILANA	German wirehaired pointers
ILENE	American shorthairs
ILLIAD	When 'Elliot' won't do
ILLUSION	When you believe that they've actually gotten trained, but they haven't
ILLUSTRATOR	A pet for an advertising director
ILSE	Swedish shepherds
ILYA	Russian shorthairs, Korats
IMAGINE	A peaceful pet
IMMIGRANT	A foreign pet
IMMUNITY	For someone in the witness protection program
IMMY	Immunity's code name
IMOGENE	For a cocoa-colored pet
IMP	Yorkies
IMPERIAL HIGHNESS	Angoras

IMPLORER	For a pet that's always begging
IMPLYER	For a pet that won't just tell it like it is
IMPORTED	For a foreign breed
IMPORTER	For the person who brought over the imported breed
IMPOSTER	For the pet that pretends to be imported
IMPRESSER	For the pet that pretends to be imported in order to impress
IMPRESSIVE	For the pet that actually is imported and is impressive
IMPULSE	Hyperactives
IMUS	Early morning pets
INA	Miniature schnauzers
INCA	For a builder
INCH	Snakes
INCORPORATED	For someone with a new pet and a new business
INCUBATOR	You got a preemie
INDEPENDENCE DAY	Borzois, Yugoslavian border hounds, Bosnian hounds
INDEX	For an organized pet
INDI	A pet that likes adventure
INDIA	Your pet has a spot on its forehead
INDIA INK	A black pet
INDIAN	A feathered pet
INDIAN SUMMER	Shaded goldens
INDIANA	American foxhounds
INDIANA JONES	See Indi
INDIC	Wetterhouns
INDICATOR	For a pet that gives you a hint before biting
INDIGO	Blue pets
INDIRA	For a female leader of pets
INDISCREET	Tomcats

INDOCHINE	Siamese
INDOOR	My cat, Homer . . . the only outdoor cat who comes inside to go to the bathroom
INERTIA	Your pet won't move unless provoked
INES	Catalan sheepdogs
IN EXCESS	Any pet over 200 lbs.
INEXHAUSTIBLE	Dandie Dinmont terriers . . . actually, most terriers
INEZ	Fabulous pet name
INFERNO	A towering pet
INFIELDER	Ball chasers
INFINITI	You want one
INFLICTER	Pit bulls, Dobermans, Rottweilers, etc.
INFLIGHT	Birds
INFORMANT	Parrots
INFORMER	Parakeets
INFRADIP	Pets that like to swim
INFRARED	Bats
INGMAR	A director's pet
INGLEBERT	Javanese, Burmese, Tonkinese
INGOT	You have a pet that's as good as gold
INGRAM	You listen to WCBS
INGRES	Your pet refuses to go outdoors
INGRID	Swiss hounds
INGROWN	A podiatrist's pet
INKBERRY	Black-and-white Persians
INKBLOTZ	A psychiatrist's pet
INKLE	American curls
INKLING	You don't quite get it . . . why was it that you wanted this pet?
INKSPOT	A printer's pet
INKWELL	Black Bombays
INNER CIRCLE	Your pet's in the in-crowd
INNER CITY	You have a city pet
INNER SPACE	Your pet is very Zen

INNESS	A painter's pet
INNIE	Outie's brother
INNING	You love baseball
INNIS	A pet for a Roy
INOCULATOR	A doctor's pet
INPUT	A computer operator's pet
INQUIRER	A gossip's pet
INSIDE OUT	Devon rexes, sphinxes
INSIDE TRACK	Greyhounds
INSIDER	A trader's pet
INSOLE	Another pet for a podiatrist
INSOMNIA	A nocturnal pet
INSOMNIAC	For an aggressive nocturnal pet
INSOOK LEE	Chinese Imperial Ch'n, Chow Chows, Lhasa Apsos
INSPECTOR	For a Clouseau fan
INSPIRATION	An artist's pet
INSTALLER	A Cable TV man's pet
INSTALLMENT PLAN	An expensive pet
INSTINCT	Your basic pet
INSTRUCTOR	A bossy pet
INSURANCE	Instead of a burglar alarm
INSURED	How Insurance makes you feel
INTEGRATED	Black-and-white pets
INTERIM	The pet you buy before having the baby
INTERLOPER	For a pet that constantly jumps in bed with you at the wrong moments
INTERMEZZO	An opera lover's pet
INTERNAL REVENUE	An auditor's pet
INTERNATIONAL	Good name for a mutt
INTERPOL	A spy's pet
INTERROGATOR	For a Staffordshire bull terrier . . . your simple pit bull type

INTESTINE	Snakes
INTREPID	A sailor's pet
INTRO	Your first pet
INTUITION	A psychic's pet
INVENTOR	A storyteller's pet
INVESTOR	A pet for a Wall Street tycoon
INVISIBLE MAN	For the pet who's never there when you want it . . . and IS when you don't
IODINE	Red pets
IONESCO	A playwright's pet . . . on the absurd side
IOTA	Any of the mini breeds
IPANEMA	It's tall, and tan, and young and lovely, the girl from Ipanema goes walking
IRA	Your pet looks like an accountant
IRELAND	Any of the Irish breeds
IRENE	American foxhounds
IRENEE	American foxhound with a whine
IRIS	An ophthalmologist's pet
IRISH	Irish wolfhounds
IRISH STEW	The wolfhound's litter
IRMA	American wirehairs
IRMA LA DOUCE	Longhaired dachshunds
IRON	A bulldog that likes to flex his muscles
IRON AGE	For the bulldog that's a little old-fashioned
IRON CURTAIN	For the bulldog that's out of touch
IRON HORSE	For the bulldog that thinks it's Lou Gehrig
IRON JOHN	For the bulldog that knows he's a real man
IRON MAN	For a bulldog that lifts weights
IRON WILL	For the bulldog that's won the battle over who's master
IRON WOOD	For the bulldog that golfs

IRONCLAD	For the bulldog you'll never get out of owning
IRONSIDES	For the bulldog that wants to be a policeman
IRONWEED	For a mutt that aspires to be a bulldog
IRONY	For the bulldog you didn't want but now you love
IROQUOIS	American eagles
IRS	You're constantly audited
IRV	Irving's nickname
IRVING	What a fabulous name for a pet
IRVIS	The father was Irving and the mother was Mavis
IRWIN	Also a good name for any pet
ISAAC	For a mellow cat
ISABELL	For the parrot that chimes in
ISABELLA	A pet that likes explorers
ISADORA	A lovely, independent cat
ISADORA DUNCAN	For a cat that leaps, or a dunker (a dog from Norway)
ISAIAH	Any pets that foretell the future
ISHERWOOD	Any pet that treats life as a cabaret
ISHIKAWA	Japanese bobtails, Japanese spitzes
ISHKABIBBLE	A pet that's too cute for a real name
ISHMAEL	For a whale watcher
ISHTAR	For a camel watcher
ISIDORE	It thinks it's a door
ISLAND QUEEN	A pet from Manhattan
ISLEY	Your pet has 'lost that lovin' feeling'
ISOLDA	A salesman's pet
ISSEY	For a Cockney, hissing animal
ISUZU	Your pet would say anything to make a sale
ITALIAN STALLION	You got a horse from Italy
ITCH	An allergic person's pet

ITCHY	A prickly pet
ITHACA	You like cold winters
ITURBI	A concert pianist's pet
IVAN	For a male pet who's terrible, but not that terrible
IVAN THE TERRIBLE	For a male pet who IS that terrible
IVANA	For a female pet who's terrible, but not that terrible
IVANA THE TERRIBLE	For the female pet who IS that terrible
IVANHOE	I read it but don't remember what it was about
IVES	A burly pet
IVOR	Russian wolfhounds, borzois, Russian blues
IVORY	For any white pet where a tusk is a plus
IVY	Boston terriers
IVY LEAGUE	Boston terriers with credentials
IYAH	An Israeli pet
IZAAK	Oysters
IZOD	For a preppie pet . . . unless you have an alligator
IZZY	Pets partial to homemade chicken soup

J. EDGAR	American bloodhounds
JABBA	For a big, fat pet
JABBAR	For a basketball fan
JABBERWOCKY	For a Lewis Carroll fan
JABOT	A pet with a crest of white hair at the neck
JACK	The most frequently used name for the Jack Russell terrier
JACK BENNY	A penny-pinching Jack Russell
JACK FROST	A northern Jack Russell
JACK LONDON	A literary Jack Russell
JACKHAMMER	A loud Jack Russell
JACKIE	A female Jack Russell
JACKKNIFE	A tough Jack Russell
JACKPOT	A gambler's Jack Russell
JACKRABBIT	A quick Jack Russell
JACKO	A circus Jack Russell
JACKSON	A Browne Jack Russell
JACOB	A religious Jack Russell
JACOBY	A litigious Jack Russell . . . pair with Meyers

JACQUARD	A Jack Russell into fabric
JACQUELINE	A formal Jacqueline Russell
JACQUETTA	A Spanish Jack Russell
JACUZZI	A Jack Russell that appreciates the good life
JADE	Any of your green pets . . . turtles, snakes, frogs
JADED	Any of your green pets that have been around
JAEGER	English setters . . . well-dressed and sporty
JAFFEE	For a Sam or a Rona
JAGGER	You're a Rolling Stones fan
JAI ALAI	A Spanish mastiff who fetches
JAIME	Non-pedigree blue and white shorthairs
JAKE	One of my favorites . . . for humans as well as animals
JALAPENO	This one's a pepper
JALOPY	Floppy pets or ones that love to ride in the car
JAM	A musician's pet
JAM SESSION	A musician's brood
JAMAL	Rhodesian ridgebacks
JAMBALAYA	Mixed breeds
JAMBOREE	Your pet likes to march
JAMEEL	You're a basketball fan
JAMES	A formal pet
JAMES BOND	A spy pet
JAMES BROWN	A singing pet
JAMES DEAN	A rebel pet
JAMIE	A halfhearted rebel pet
JAMMER	A windy pet
JAMMIES	Your pet sleeps a lot
JAMSHID	Early legendary king of Persia
JAN	Pair with Dean

JANA	Pyrenees mastiffs . . . big and powerful . . . friendly and don't eat much
JANE	See Jane. See Jane run. Pair with Dick
JANE DOE	For a pet from the humane society
JANE EYRE	A pet with a sense of melodrama and expressive eyes . . . pair with Mr. Rochester
JAYNE MANSFIELD	For a young bichon frise
JANE MARPLE	For an old bloodhound
JANEANE	You're into double single names
JANET	For a good, reliable animal . . . one that won't let you down
JANGLE	Tennessee treeing brindles
JANGLES	Mr. Bo
JANICE	Another old high school friend
JANIE	An old elementary school friend
JANOVIC	You're into decorating
JANUARY	For an Aquarian
JANUARY MAN	Police dogs
JANUS	Guard dogs
JAPHETH	Son of Noah
JARGON	Mixed breeds
JARRAH	It's an Australian tree . . . for one of your larger breeds
JARRED	Trigg hounds . . . created in Kentucky for hunting
JARRUS	Hovawarts . . . run easily over difficult terrain
JARVIS	Black-and-tan coonhounds
JASMINE	Basenjis, poodles, Angoras
JASON	For the pet with a golden fleece
JASPER	A Johns pet
JASSID	For a pet that likes arid, hot climates
JASTROW	Chesapeake Bay retrievers
JAT	A pet for a Punjab

JAVA	For someone who loves coffee or any dark brown pet
JAWS	Nice for a Rottweiler or fish
JAY	Jaybirds
JAYBIRD	Blue jays, Mexican hairless, Devon rex (also hairless)
JAYNE	A fancy Jane
JAZEMOND	A pet with airs
JAZMINE	A pet that smells good
JAZZ	For a hot, cool pet
JD	Delinquent pets
JEAN	For a pet in its prime
JEAN-MARIE	A parochial school pet
JEANETTE	Torties and white Scottish folds
JEANNIE	I dream of . . .
JEANS	For any of the blue pets
JEDI	Your pet battles interstellar evil
JEDI KNIGHT	Dobermans, Rottweilers, Newfoundlands
JEDIDIAH	You have a peaceful pet
JEEP	Your pet is willing to travel anywhere
JEEVES	Doubles as your butler
JEFFERSON	A presidential pet
JEFFREY	Jefferson's nickname
JEHOSOPHAT	Pet frogs
JEKYLL	Pair with Hyde
JELLO	Pudgy, roly-poly pets
JELLY	Cuddly, soft, fat pets
JELLY BEAN	A pet for Ronald Regan
JELLY ROLL	Dachshunds
JEMMY	Oriental reds
JENA	Somerset harriers
JENKINS	Sounds more like a butler
JENNELL	Swedish shepherds
JENNINGS	It watches the evening news with you
JENNY	Malteses, goldens, tabbies

JENSEN	You like silverware or your name is George
JEOPARDY	Either you love the game show, or, you have a guard dog
JEREMIA	Was a bullfrog
JEREMIAH	Was a good friend of mine
JEREMY	For a pet with its irons in the fire
JERMAINE	For a singing and dancing pet
JEROME	Old English sheepdogs, Scottish terriers, Maine coons
JERRELL	Wild Abyssinians
JERRY	Tom & Jerry were my friend's two beagles in Mamaroneck . . . now she has Barnum & Bailey
JESSE	My own wonderful son
JESSE JAMES	You have a rascal
JESSEL	A comedian and toastmaster's pet
JESSUP	Pyrenees mastiffs
JESTER	For a Maltese with a bow in its hair
JET	Black pets
JET LAG	Your pet sleeps a lot
JET SET	You have three Afghans
JETH	Tawny boxers
JETHRO	You have a Beverly Hillbilly
JETSAM	Another pet from the pound
JETTY	Portuguese or Irish water dogs
JEWEL	A priceless pet
JEWELS	Even more priceless than Jewel
JEZEBEL	For your female flirting pet
JEZEBELL	For a very forward, nondiscriminatory pet
JIANG	Shih Tzus, Lhasas, Chows
JIFFY	Pets that race
JIGS	Work dogs
JIGSAW	You have a puzzling pet

JIING DONG	Lhasa Apsos, Japanese bobtails
JILL	Pair for a Jack Russell terrier
JILLIAN	California spangleds
JIM DANDY	A pet who's an excellent example of its breed
JIMENEZ	For José
JIMINEY CRICKET	You loved Pinocchio
JIMMY	For a pet with a large beak or a very long snout
JIMMY STEWART	Afghans, salukis, Great Danes . . . tall, thin pets
JINX	Black cats
JITTERBUG	Chihuahuas, toy poodles, or anything else small and hyper
JO	One of the Little Women
JO JO	Jo's pet name
JOAN OF ARC	Not so happy days
JOANIE	*Happy Days*
JOB	A pet with problems
JOBBER	A middleman's pet
JOBLESS	A pure luxury pet
JOCASTA	Queen of Thebes and mother of Oedipus
JOCK	An athlete's pet
JOCKEY	For a pet that likes to go to the races
JODHPUR	For a pet that likes to go to the races and wear pants
JODHPURR	For a cat that likes to go to the races and wear pants
JODI	Pekingese, Scotties, Welch corgis
JOE	For a dependable pet like Janet
JOE LEWIS	You love boxing
JOE MONTANA	You love football
JOE PALOOKA	A fictional pet for a boxing fan
JOEL	You have a gray pet

JOEY	American shorthairs, Tennessee treeing brindles
JOFFREY	You love ballet
JOHN	Another for the American breeds
JOHN DOE	Another pet from the pound
JOHN HANCOCK	It leaves its signature when left alone too often
JOHN HENRY	A steel-driving pet
JOHNNY	Your pet drinks out of the toilet
JOHNNY ON THE SPOT	Your pet is well trained
JOHNNY-COME-LATELY	Your pet is not well trained
JOHNSON	Turkish Vans
JOIE	A happy French pet
JOIE DE VIVRE	A happy French pet that loves life
JOINT CHIEF	Bulldogs, brindle boxers, tawny boxers
JOJOBA	Clean pets
JOKER	A parrot with its own repertoire
JOLLY	For a happy American pet
JOLLY RANCHER	For a happy American pet with a ranch
JOLLY ROGER	For a happy Roger, with or without the ranch
JOLSON	He loves his mammy
JON JON	For a small Jon
JONAH	The largest fish in the tank
JONAS	Your pet believes in vaccines
JONATHAN	Once a rarely seen breed. Now, everyone has one
JONES	For a pet that likes to use an alias
JONESES	A pet you try to keep up with
JONESIE	A pet you're immediately comfortable with
JONG	Your pet has a fear of flying
JONQUIL	Yellow-haired pets

JOON	Japanese bobtails
JOPLIN	American longhairs
JORDACHE	A jeans person's pet
JORDAN	Pair with Marsh . . . a shopper's pet
JORDANA	A Jackie Collins character
JORDIE	For a small shopper
JOREL	Pair with Superman
JORGE	A Spanish George
JOSÉ	A Spanish Joe
JOSÉ JIMENEZ	My name . . .
JOSEPH	Your pet dreams in Technicolor
JOSEPHINA	A Spanish Josephine
JOSEPHINE	An English Josephina
JOSETTE	French bulldogs
JOSHUA	Colorpointed European Devon rexes
JOSLYN	Longhaired Angoras
JOSS	For someone who believes in luck
JOSYLEN	A luck lady
JOURNEYMAN	A traveler's pet
JOWLS	Basset hounds and bulldogs
JOY	A happy pet
JOYCE	A happy pet that writes
JOYCLYN	A happy pet that brings good fortune
JOYFUL	A happy pet that brings good fortune and good health
JOYRIDE	Your pet is large enough for your child to ride on
JUAN	A Spanish John
JUAN CARLOS	King of Spain
JUANITA	A Spanish Jane
JUÁREZ	Mexican national hero 1806–1872
JUBILEE	You received this pet for a big anniversary
JUDAH	For a Maccabee
JUDAS	Pit bulls

JUDD	A country singer's pet
JUDE	Hey
JUDGE	A pet for a juror
JUDITH	Cary Grant would never have been able to repeat it three times in a row like 'Judy'
JUDO	For a martial arts buff
JUDSON	Judd's full name
JUDY	Judy, Judy, Judy!
JUGHEAD	You've read all the Archie comics
JUGO	For someone into juice (Sp.)
JUICER	For someone into health food
JUILLIARD	For someone into arts
JUJUBEE	For someone into junk food
JUKEBOX	For someone into the '50s
JULEP	For someone into mint drinks
JULES	For someone into Feiffer
JULIA	For someone into Roberts
JULIANA	Egyptian maus
JULIET	Romeo, oh, Romeo . . .
JULIO	Springer spaniels . . . I like the incongruity of it
JULIUS	For someone into the color orange
JULIUS CAESAR	For someone into power
JULY	For a July baby
JUMBO	For a big baby
JUMP SHOT	You play basketball
JUMPING JACK	Another Jack Russell terrier name
JUNE	For a June baby
JUNG	For someone into psychoanalysis
JUNGLE JIM	For a Jim that likes to hike
JUNGLE SPIRIT	For a Jim that used to hike
JUNIUS	I don't get it myself
JUNO	Alaskan malamutes
JUPITER	You're a *Northern Exposure* fan

JURA	Turkish Vans
JURASSIC	Frogs, lizards, snakes
JUROR	A trial attorney's pet
JURY	A trial attorney with more than one pet
JUSTIN	Harlequin Great Danes (also my eldest son's proper name)
JUSTIN THYME	Harlequin Great Danes that like to cook
JUSTINE	Female Harlequin Great Danes
JUTE	Hey

K'FULLE	You have to watch it all the time
K.C.	Either a pet from Kansas City, short for 'Kitty Cat', or a pet with a sunshine band
KABUKI	A silent pet with a white face
KÁDÁR	For a Hungarian Communist
KAFKA	Borzois, Russian blues
KAHLIL	Pharaoh hounds
KAHLÚA	An after dinner pet
KAHUNA	Hawaiian pets
KAISER	You have a German shepherd or else you like the rolls
KALB	A journalist's pet
KALEIDOSCOPE	For your fish tank
KALI	Collies
KALIB	Another Pharaoh hound
KALMUK	Mongolian language
KAMA	Hindu god of love
KAMALI	For a very with-it, trend-setting pet
KAMIKAZE	Hyperactive pets

KAN KAN	Dancing French poodles
KANDINSKY	A painter's pet
KANDYMAN	A chocoholic's pet
KANE	You like watching *Kung Fu . . . The Legend Continues*
KANNADA	A language from southern India
KANSAS	You have a cairn terrier and plan to move
KAPPA	For a fraternity aficionado
KARA	Mia mine
KARAMAZOV	For brothers
KARATE	You're into the martial arts
KARATE KID	The child of the martial arts aficionado
KAREEM	Better than milk for your cat
KARL	The name of my son's enormous amplifier
KARLOFF	Pair with Boris
KARLOS	A fancy Carlos
KARMA	The pet that was meant to be
KAROL	A fancy Carol
KARRAS	Very big pets
KARTIK	Hindu month
KARUS	A character from *Bambi*
KASBAH	Rock the Casbah, rock the Casbah
KASEY	A fancy Casey
KASHA	For a Varnisha (Kasha Varnisha is a noodle dish)
KASHMIR	The territory, not the cloth
KASPER	A designer's pet
KASPI	For someone with fond memories of the Caspian Sea
KASSANDRA	A beautiful, full, fluffy feline
KASSIE	Longhaired calicos, Yorkshire terriers, pulis
KAT	A fancy Cat

KATARINA	Russian blue longhairs
KATCH	Your pet likes to play ball
KATE	Katherine's nickname
KATEEBA	Egyptian mau shorthairs, Orientals
KATERINA	Another for the Russian breeds
KATHERINE	American breeds
KATIE	American non-pedigree shorthairs
KATMANDOO	A male cat's litter box
KATO	A pet that's a real trial
KATONA	Beagles, Bernese mountain dogs
KATRINA	Borzois . . . docile and extremely loyal
KATSINETTES	It can dance flamenco
KATSUMI	Just what you don't want your cat to do
KATZ	For a dog
KAVA	The beginnings of a trip to the dentist
KAVANAGH	Irish setters without cavities
KAVIDA	A dentist's pet
KAY	Cairn terriers, Yorkies, wirehair fox terriers
KAYAK	Alaskan malamutes, Eskimo dogs
KAYE	For a Danny fan (1913–1987)
KAYOED	Boxers
KAZZI	Chocolate tortie Persians
KEANU	Speedy pets
KEATON	For a Buster, Diane, or Michael
KEATS	Poet
KEELER	For a boater . . . a dancer . . . or someone into Rubies
KEEN	You loved the '50s
KEEPER	When you weren't sure, but, went for it
KEFAUVER	For a political animal
KEFIR	A drink made from fermented cow's milk
KEGLER	A bowler's pet
KEIKO	Japanese bobtails

KELB	Means 'dog' in Arabic
KELLOGG	For a serial pet
KELLY	Irish springers, Irish terriers
KELVIN	Blue Korats
KEMP	A champion
KEN	Pair with Barbie
KENDALL	Pets that looks like a Ken doll
KENDL	An altered Ken doll pet
KENDRIX	The Ken doll pet that does tricks
KENJI	Japanese spitz, Japanese bobtails
KENNETH	For an aspiring hairdresser
KENO	À la Bingo
KENT	An aspiring duke or duchess's pet
KENTON	Sussex spaniels
KENTUCKY	You like racing
KENTUCKY BLUE GRASS	You really like racing
KENTUCKY DERBY	For very fast horses
KENTUCKY WOMAN	For very fast Neil Diamond fans
KENYA	You identify with the NY Marathon winner
KENYATTA	Kenya's first president (1964–1978)
KENZO	A designing pet
KERBY	For Cosmo Topper fans
KERMAN	It reminds you of a Persian rug
KERMIT	For any of the green pets
KERNEL	For a teeny-weeny pet
KERRIA	Croatian sheepdogs
KERRY	English sheepdogs
KERRY BLUE	For the cat
KETCH	Retrievers
KETCHUP	Red pets, or ones that are always late

KEVIN	Your pet likes Bacon
KEWPIE DOLL	An Angora . . . what could be kewpier?
KEYBOARD	A pianist's pet
KEYNOTE	A speaker's pet
KEYS	A musician's pet
KGB	A spy's pet
KHAFRE	Egyptian pharaohs
KHAKI	American army pets
KHALID	King of Saudi Arabia
KHALKHA	Official language of the Mongolian People's Republic
KHASHOGGI	You're hoping it will be rich one day
KHOMEINI	This is the worst pet you ever had
KHRUSHCHEV	Your pet likes shoes
KIBBEE	It likes Arabic food
KIBBI	For a little round, puffy dog, like a bischon frise
KICKING BEAR	Bernese mountain dogs, Newfoundlands . . . something really BIG
KIDD	Young pets
KIDDER	For someone very Margo
KIDDISH	For a pet that acts young, or one that likes to eat Saturday afternoons
KIER	Saint Bernards seem to get all the 'liquor' names
KIERKEGAARD	Philosophic pets
KILDARE	Your pet aspires to be a doctor
KILEY	Australian terriers . . . lively, spirited, and dignified
KILO	A dieter's or weight lifter's pet
KILROY	Was here
KIM	A jungle animal (see Kipling)
KIMOSABE	Tonto's pet name for the Lone Ranger
KING	You have a big animal
KING CHARLES	Try as it might, it will remain a prince

KING EDWARD	English mastiffs
KING GEORGE	Harlequin Great Danes
KING HUSSEIN	Neapolitan mastiffs
KING KONG	Pugs
KING LEAR	Another one for the pug, because the eyes are so big
KING LOUIS	For your 14th pet
KING SIZE	English mastiffs
KINGFISH	From the *Amos & Andy* TV series
KINSKI	Nastassia and Klaus . . . for when you've kept the offspring
KIOWA	Blue Tonkinese
KIPLING	Gunga Din, Rudyard, Kim
KIPLINGER	You're into newsletters
KIPPY	Smooth collies
KIRI	Field spaniels . . . hardy and fast, sweet and affectionate
KIRK	For a Trekkie
KIRKPATRICK	For an ambassador
KIRKWOOD	Funny cats
KIRSTEN	For a pet that will eventually make a debut
KIRSTIE ALLEY	*Cheers!*
KISHI	Lhasa Apsos
KISHKA	Another name for hyperactive pets
KISMET	For the pet that was meant to be
KISSES	For a pet that loves to lick
KISSINGER	German shorthaired pointers
KIT	For a *Night Rider* fan
KITT	For an Earthy pet
KITTEN	Actually, a very sweet name . . . Kathy's nickname from *Father Knows Best*
KITTY	For *Gunsmoke* fans
KITTY HAWK	Flying cats

KITUBAH	For a pet that plans to marry and keep the receipt
KIVI	For someone into fruit or shoe polish with an accent
KIWI	For someone into fruit or shoe polish—no accent
KLAUS	For someone into Germans
KLEE	For someone into art
KLEIST	For someone into poetry
KLEMPERER	For someone into *Hogan's Heroes*
KLINGER	For someone into *M*A*S*H*
KLONDIKE	For someone into ice cream bars
KLUTE	For a detective
KNICK	For a pet that can jump through hoops
KNICKERBOCKER	For a pet that can jump through hoops and drink beer at the same time
KNIEVEL	For an evil pet
KNIGHT RIDER	A pet that will be out at night
KNISH	Your pet eats fried, mashed potatoes
KNOCKWURST	Dachshunds
KNOEDLER	An art lover's pet
KNOX	For a pet with good strong nails
KOCCHI	Italian pointers
KOCH	It plans to run for mayor one day
KODACHROME	A photographer's pet
KODAK	You have a picture perfect pet
KOKOLADA	You like to vacation in the islands
KONFEWSHUN	Your pet definitely has attention deficit problems
KONG	A big, hairy pet
KOOKY	For a crazy pet
KOOLKAT	Just what it says
KOPPEL	For a pet that needs a new hairstyle
KORNELIA	An ophthalmologist's pet
KORNY	A pet with eye problems

KOUFAX	For any pet that can make a record number of strikeouts in one season
KOWTOW	A yes-man's pet
KRAKATOA	A big pet that steps on your foot all the time
KRAMER	For Seinfeld fans
KRAUS	German pets
KREFELD	A small town in Germany where I lived the first year I was married
KREPLACH	Yiddish pets
KRIS	See Kristofferson
KRISPIE	For a pet into rice cakes
KRISSIE	From *Three's Company*
KRISTIE	Irish terriers
KRISTIE ALLEY	Alley cats
KRISTOFF	Christoff with a K . . . Someone into silver
KRISTOFFERSON	A name that will only appear on its pedigree papers . . . otherwise, it's Kris to the family
KROOK	Your pet steals
KROONER	Parrots
KRUPA	You love music as well as jeans
KUBLAI KHAN	For any of the Chinese pets with a talent for running an empire
KUBRICK	You're looking forward to the year 2001
KURALT	Your pet that likes to travel around the United States
KURTZ	Swoosie Kurtz . . . now, there's a name for you!
KYM	For a Kim that likes to go to the gym, for a swim, with him and Jim
KYOTO	For any of the Japanese breeds

LA FEMME NIKITA	For a female that REALLY knows how to take care of herself.
LA LA	I actually know someone named La La. It's so cute.
LABELLE	A beautiful French pointer
LABOW	Hogan's French friend
LACE	Cavalier King Charles spaniels, Himalayans, Gordon setters
LACES	For the cat that's always playing with your shoes
LACEY	Pair with Cagney
LACOYNA	Croatian sheepdogs
LAD	Male collie
LADDIE	Male collie's son
LADDIE BOY	Male Collie's son with Irish eyes
LADIBYRD	No, it's not named after the former First Lady
LADY	Pair with Tramp
LADY BIRD	This one is

LADY CHATTERLEY	A pet who sleeps with you
LADY DI	A pet with a lot of baggage at the moment
LADY JANE	Old English mastiffs
LADY MACBETH	Dalmatians (Out damned spot!)
LAFAYETTE	French poodles, French bulldogs
LAFITTE	An expensive pet
LAGERFELD	A designer's pet
LAILA	Will ease your worried mind
LAKE	Portuguese water dogs, Irish water dogs
LAMARR	For a Hedy pet
LAMB	Bedlington terriers
LAMBCHOP	For someone who grew up with Shari Lewis
LAMBIE PIE	For someone who grew up with my mother
LAMOUR	For someone in love with love
LANCASTER	You like to go for midnight swims
LANCE	Lancelot's nickname
LANCELOT	You loved *Camelot*
LAND ROVER	For a family that has the car and the pet that roams free
LANDERS	Your pet gives advice
LANDON	For a pet that thinks it's a pilot
LANDY	Lakeland terriers . . . affectionate, cheerful, and stubborn
LANG	For a Ronettes fan . . . Do lang, do lang, do lang
LANGFORD	Viszlas . . . intelligent, trainable hunting dogs
LANGLEY	A CIA agent's pet
LANGSTON	A poet's pet
LANGTRY	A dog who lives west of the Rockies
LANIE	A nice, plump Himalayan
LANSBURY	For a *Murder, She Wrote* fan

LANSING	For a female movie aficionado
LANVIN	Your pet smells great
LANZA	Either you are named Mario, or you live in Mamaroneck
LAPIS	For a Blue seal point shorthair
LAPIS LAZULI	You have a gem
LAPTOP	For someone with both the cat and the computer
LAREDO	A pet with a western emphasis
LARSEN	My accountant
LASSIE	Collies and only collies
LATKA	*Taxi*
LATOYA	A pet with a lot of siblings
LAUDER	A pet with good skin
LAUGHTON	Basset hounds, English bulldogs
LAUPER	Your pet has orange hair
LAURA	An American shorthair . . . like Laura Petrie
LAURA ASHLEY	Clothes designer
LAUREL	Clothes designer
LAUREN	Clothes designer
LAURENT	Clothes designer
LAURI	Clothes wearer
LAVERNE	And Shirley
LAVIN	Another clothes designer
LAWFORD	A presidential brother-in-law type
LAWRENCE	An animal who won't loosen up
LAWRENCE OF ARABIA	Egyptian sphinx, pharaoh hounds
LAYAWAY	It was expensive
LAYOFF	For one of the non-working breeds
LAYOUT	An art designer's pet
LAZULI	Russian blues
LE CARRÉ	A spy dog

LE GRAND	A very large animal who reminds you of a sports car
LEA	Twentieth-century version of a biblical name
LEAH	A biblical name for a twentieth-century pet
LEAHY	Irish setters, Irish wolfhounds, etc.
LEAR	A Seeing Eye dog
LEARY	Heavy doses of catnip
LEE	A Confederate pet
LEEWAY	A pet for whom you keep having to make exceptions
LEFTY	An animal with two left feet
LEGEND	Any animal with a mink coat
LEHMAN	More brothers
LEIF	Norwegian elkhounds
LELAND	You're an *L.A. Law* fan
LEMONADE	For a sour puss
LENDL	For a tennis fan
LENIN	Siberian huskies, borzois
LENNON	English setters with a talent for composing
LENNY	You have a comedian
LENO	For an NBC late nighter
LENYA	For a Lotte
LEO	For a large cat or pet born in August
LEON	One of the great names
LEONA	From rags to riches to the pen
LEONARD	My lawyer
LEONARDO	A Teenage Mutant Ninja Turtle or someone into real art
LEONORE	Flat-coated retrievers
LEOTA	Iceland dogs . . . lively, affectionate, and active
LESLIE	An animal of indeterminate gender
LESTER	My friend's psychoanalyst

LETTERMAN	For a CBS late nighter
LETTY	A feminist's pet
LEVANT	Talented but alcoholic
LEVI'S	Blue pets
LEWIS	And Clark . . . likes to explore the neighborhood
LIABLE	An attorney's pet
LIAM	Big and beautiful
LIBBY	You prefer canned peas to fresh
LIBERACE	A pet with great flair and panache
LIBERTY	Truth, justice, and the American way
LICHTENSTEIN	A painter's pet
LICKERISH	For the pet that thinks that you're the candy
LICORICE	A candy lover's pet
LIGHTFOOT	For that pet that manages to sneak up on you every time
LIGHTNING	Female half of a Great Dane couple (see Thunder)
LI'L ABNER	A backwoods pet
LILAC	Smells like a room freshener
LILAH	Lilac lynx point Javanese longhairs
LILI	High Lili, high low
LILITH	*Cheers* and *Frasier* . . . pit bulls
LILY	A pet of the valley
LIMA BEAN	A pet that's good for you
LIMBAUGH	For a big, opinionated pet . . . preferably Republican
LIMBO	For a pet unsure of its next move
LIMOGES	Delicate and expensive
LIN YI	Chow Chows, Lhasa Apsos, Shih Tzus, etc.
LINCOLN	A bearded, honest pet
LINDA	The name of a good girl
LINDBERGH	Birds

LINDFORS	Better for a butler than a pet
LINDSAY	My niece . . . about to go to college
LINKLETTER	An artful pet
LINUS	A pet with a blanket
LION	Your pet's not afraid to take what it wants
LIONEL	For a male into trains
LIONELLE	For a female into trains
LIPOSUCTION	Greyhounds
LIPPI	Artist
LIPPIE	For someone into collagen injections
LIPS	Snakes, lizards
LIPSTICK	For a femme fatale
LISZT	A composer's pet
LITHGOW	An actor's pet
LITTLE BIG MAN	Pugs
LITTLE JOHN	Big John's son
LITTLE LORD FAUNTLEROY	A pet you plan to dress up
LITTLE LOTTA	Fat boxers
LITTLE RICHARD	Good golly, Miss Molly
LIVERWURST	Dalmatians
LIVINGSTON	It's always wandering off
LIZ	See Doubles
LIZA	Long legs, short hair, pedigree lineage
LIZZI	Snakes, unless you get a lizard
L.L. BEAN	For a catalog shopper
LLOYD	Basset hounds
LOAFER	For all cats
LOFTY	Your pet is full of itself
LOGAN	A pet that you picked up at Boston's airport
LOIS	Pair with Clark

LOIS LANE	Professional suffering from unrequited love
LOLA	Sexy, but not too sexy
LOLLI	Your two-year-old's pronunciation
LOLLICAT	Your three-year-old's choice
LOLLIPOP	Your four-year-old's wish
LOLLIPUP	Your self-congratulatory solution
LOLLOBRIGIDA	Everyone will know what you meant
LOMBARD	Blond and beautiful
LOMBARDI	Powerful and competitive
LOMBARDO	For a guy
LONDON	Any of the English breeds
LONGFELLOW	Dachshunds
LONGSHOT	Dachshunds who race
LONGWORTH	Dachshunds who win
LONI	Dachshunds smarter than they look
LOOFAH	Bristly pets
LOPEZ	Trini
LORD BYRON	Old English sheepdogs, English mastiffs, etc.
LOREN	Dandie Dinmont terriers . . . great mouse catchers . . . affectionate and playful
LORENZO	My cousin Ruth's new husband . . . they just moved to Buenos Aires
LORETTA	Young silver patched tabbies
LORRE	For a Peter
LOTTE	Lenya
LOU ELLA	Happens to be a matchmaker in NYC
LOU ELLEN	Happens to be a client
LOUIE	You'd better love the song
LOUIS	Would like to be a client
LOUIS VUITTON	Your pet will have LV LV LV LV LV all over its collar
LOUISA MAY	For Alcott fans

LOUISE	The Pekingese . . . great pet name . . . makes it seem human
LOUPI	Pulis
LOVE	As long as it's not what you call anyone else in the family
LOVE BUG	For a Herbie
LOVECHILD	A coupling you never approved of but couldn't prevent. Perfect for mutts
LOVEJOY	For a pet into antiques and mysteries
LOVEY	Shorthaired red mackerel tabbies
LOWBOY	For a short pet . . . or a depressed pet
LUCA	A pet that needs a good home
LUCAS	See Lukas
LUCCI	For a soap opera buff
LUCE	A pet that sees the light
LUCIA	My former in-laws' former neighbor
LUCIFER	For a little devil
LUCILLE	Red haired and funny
LUCINDA	Black cats
LUCKY	A pet you adopted from the pound
LUCKY LUCIANO	A hit man's pet
LUCRETIA	Borzois
LUCY	I Love Lucy . . . both the name and the show
LUDWIG	Deutsche Dogges
LUGER	A pet for someone in the NRA
LUGOSI	For a molto Bella pet
LUI LUI	"I said, ah, we gotta go"
LUIGI	Italian pointers, Italian greyhounds, French poodles, Jack Russells, dachshunds
LUKAS	Sounds like a tough guy to me
LUKE	A semiwarm pet
LUKE SKYWALKER	*Star Wars* . . . any pet that learns tricks the hard way

LULU	Blue-eyed, white Angoras . . . or else, you got a beaut
LUMET	You're a movie buff
LURCH	A pet that lopes instead of runs
LUTHER	Devilish
LYLE	Cockatoos, cockatiels
LYNDON	Definitely perfect for a basset hound
LYON	You have a big cat
LYONS	For a Swiss hound . . . as in the town

MA KETTLE	For an old, skinny pet married to Pa
MABEL	I don't know why, but I love this name for a pet
MACARONI	Your pet's a real noodle
MACAROON	Persian tortoiseshells
MACARTHUR	A pet that likes the park
MACAW	Hanover hounds . . . search out game . . . obedient and affectionate
MACBETH	'Out damned spot!' I guess we know what happened at this house
MACGREGOR	Scottish terriers
MACHO MAN	Pugs, boxers, bulldogs
MAC IVOR	A pet that knows how to use his hands
MACK	Any pet you feel very familiar with
MACK THE KNIFE	I was in seventh grade and learned to dance to this song . . . and a BOY actually said that I looked pretty
MACKENZIE	Scottish folds, Scottish terriers
MACKINTOSH	Your pet loves the rain
MACLEISH	A pet that doesn't need a leash

MAC MURRAY	A pet for someone with three sons
MADAME BOVARY	You love Flaubert
MADELINE	Two Madelines come to mind. The famous one from Paris . . . and another one of my mother's friends
MADISON	You adore shopping
MADONNA	You think it will be a flamboyant superstar when it grows up
MAE	A big fat cat . . . I don't think Mae West would mind
MAFIA	A tough-guy pet
MAGEE	Springer spaniels, Irish setters, Irish wolfhounds
MAGELLAN	Fish
MAGGIE	Such a sweet name for a pet
MAGIC	This one speaks for itself
MAGNOLIA	A lovely tree that blossoms early spring . . . also very messy
MAGNUM	Who can look at this word and not think of Tom Selleck? Not me
MAHLER	Composer
MAID MARIAN	Pair with Robin Hood
MAILER	A postman's pet
MAINE MAN	It's from Maine. Perfect for a Maine coon
MAINLINE	Sounds like a bloodhound
MAJOR	When the decision wasn't easy
MAJOR LEAGUE	Any pet that costs over $400
MALCOME	Irish wolfhounds
MALCOLM X	Bullmastiffs
MALIBU	Pets that love the ocean, as well as the elements
MALLORY	You have family ties
MALTED	Fluffy cats. Or, Maltese
MALTESE FALCON	What else? A Maltese

MAMBO	Another good name for a Dachshund
MAMIE	Pair with Ike
MAMMA	You were upset that your child said DADA first
MANDRAKE	A plant with purplish to white flowers
MANET	Artist
MANFRED	German hunting terriers, German pointers
MANGO	Sloppy pets
MANLY	German shepherds, Rottweilers, Great Danes
MANNA	For the best pet you ever had in your life
MANNY	Smooth fox terriers
MANOLO	Portuguese water dogs . . . they are nonallergic, by the way
MANSFIELD	Jayne comes to mind, but Mansfield is a wonderful name for a male pet
MANTRA	Your pet keeps repeating the same sound over and over
MAO TSE-TUNG	Your pet leans to the far left
MAPLE SUGAR	Definitely a cat's name
MARATHON	A runner's pet
MARATHON MAN	Pet for a runner afraid of dentists
MARBLE	A sculptor's or tileman's pet
MARCELLO	Italian pointers, Italian greyhounds
MARCO	Black-and-tan coonhounds
MARCO POLO	A polo-playing black-and-tan coonhound
MARDI GRAS	A colorful cat
MARGARET	Abyssinians or tawny Great Danes
MARGUERITE	My aunt . . . mother of Nina, Danny, and Joyce . . . wife of Zaki
MARIE ANTOINETTE	A pet with a good head on its shoulders
MARIGOLD	Persian reds, golden retrievers
MARIK	It's a family name

MARILYN	My sister-in-law in New Rochelle
MARINADE	Persian shaded silver-shaded goldens
MARIO	There are several options here—my mechanic and Cuomo are two
MARIO ANDRETTI	Grand Prix champ
MARKER	Definitely for a male
MARKS	Dalmatians
MARLEE	Cats, gerbils
MARLO	You know it will be watching Donahue reruns
MARLOWE	A detective's pet
MARMALADE	Wonderful cat's name
MARS	For a pet into bars
MARSHALL	A law enforcement agent's pet
MARSHMALLOW	A white, fluffy pet
MARTHA'S VINEYARD	You want to be constantly reminded of a peaceful vacation
MARTIN	For a pet with a sheen
MARTY	A butcher's pet, from the Bronx
MARVIN	My very first boyfriend (8th grade)
MARY	A pet you can always count on
MARY JANE	A pet into shoes with straps
MARY POPPINS	Birds, Saint Bernards
MARYLOU	Whippets
MARZIPAN	You have a sweet pet that's shaped like a fruit
MASCOT	Small gray elk dogs . . . any of the minis
MASH	For those *M*A*S*H* diehards
MASON	A Mason Reese or Perry Mason fan's pet
MASTER	Your pet has the upper hand
MATA HARI	A female spy's pet
MATCHMAKER	For the unusual-looking pet you get to walk with you in the park in order to attract attention
MATHERS	For a Beaver

MATILDA	For a pet who . . . takes your money and runs Venezuela. EVERYBODY!
MATISSE	A painter's pet
MATLOCK	You have a gray pet that never changes its clothes
MATT	A pet whose coat doesn't shine
MATZOH	For a pet that's not quite cooked
MAUDE	It always reminds me of Bea Arthur in the 1970s show *Maude.* A Great Pyrenees would be good
MAUI	Hawaiian pets
MAUREEN	Any of the Irish breeds
MAURICE	Any of the French breeds
MAURY	Would have to be a pair with Connie
MAVERICK	Another one of the shows I used to love to watch with my grandmother
MAX	Tennessee treeing brindles
MAX HEADROOM	For the taller breeds . . . Irish wolfhounds, deerhounds, borzois, etc.
MAXIM'S	The great French restaurant
MAXIMILIAN	Good, strong name
MAXINE	In the same category as Maxwell
MAXWELL	Now this is an adorable name. Another one for any pet you like
MAY	You never know if it may or may not be there in the morning
MAYBELLINE	Your pet looks like it wears eyeliner
MAYA	Mexican Chihuahuas
MAYBE	For an indecisive owner
MAYBERRY	You loved *The Andy Griffith Show*
MAYDAY	Saint Bernards
MAYFLOWER	Your pet came over from England
MAYHEM	Boy, did you make the wrong choice
MAZY	Siamese
MAZZIE	This is a puzzle
McALLISTER	Scottish terriers, Scottish folds

McCLOUD	Another old TV series
McCOY	For the REAL pet
McDOOGLE	More for the Scottish breeds
McDUFF	Ends up being 'Duffy'
McENROE	You love tennis
McGEE	You tend to fib
McGILL	For an aspiring Working Woman
McGRAW	For an alley cat
McINTOSH	Either your pet loves apples or it's Irish
McKINLEY	A presidential hopeful's pet
McMILLAN	The old Rock Hudson TV show, *McMillan and Wife*
McNALLY	You love to use the atlas
McQUEEN	You still love Steve
MEAN JOE GREEN	Any of the guard dogs
MEDEA	For a pet that's not too kind to its children
MEDIA	An entertainer's pet
MEDICARE	An older pet you adopt from the pound
MEDICI	An Italian pointer from Florence, into banking and the arts
MEDOC	You love Bordeaux
MEDUSA	Your pet has very stringy, curly hair . . . pulis
MEESEKITE	Yiddish for . . . ugliness
MEG	An Australian terrier . . . about ten inches and ten pounds
MEGAN	Pomeranians . . . red fur, lively, cheerful, and bark at strangers
MEL	Was the name of our Good Humor man when I was growing up
MELBA	Peach. Yummy
MELBA TOAST	A great nighttime snack. Satisfies the need for chewing something crunchy, while not too fattening
MELLON	A financier's pet

MELLONTOES	Someone's cat is really named that
MELLOW	Great name for a hyperactive pet
MELLY	Persian chinchilla silvers
MELROSE	Your pet is addicted to evening soaps
MELVILLE	A literary pet
MELVYN	English bulldogs . . . or, your last name is Douglas
MEMO	A secretary's pet
MEMPHIS	Elvis Presley fans have an option with this
MENACHEM	A peaceful pet
MENDEL	Austrian monk & botanist (1822–84)
MENTHOL	An ex-smoker's pet
MENU	A chef's pet
MERINGUE	Birman blue points . . . (which are not blue but a meringue color)
MERIWETHER	For someone who reads the *Post*
MERLE	European blackbirds
MERLIN	A magician's pet
MERMAID	Fish
MERRILL	A cruise line captain's pet
MERRY	The happier version of Mary
MERVIN	Croatian sheepdogs, parrots, pigs
MESOPOTAMIA	Turkish vans (that's a cat, not a car)
MESSIER	You love hockey
MESSINGER	For someone into lists
METRIC	A displaced European's pet
MEW	A cat sound
MEZZO	For a short pet
MIA	Perfect for a breeding animal . . . lots of babies
MIAMI	Your pet loves the sun
MIAMI VICE	Smooth-looking police dogs
MICHELANGELO	Italian sculptor, painter, architect, and poet (1475–1564)
MICHELIN	A 'tireless' animal . . . fast on its feet

MICKEY	Good for a mouse . . . pair with Minnie
MICRODOT	Dottie would be the nickname
MICROFILM	Another pet name for a spy
MICROWAVE	Another good name for the sphinx, since it looks like it came out of a microwave
MIDAS	Rich pets or goldens
MIDAS TOUCH	Your pet will eventually be in commercials
MIDDLEBURY	A well-educated pet
MIDNIGHT	This is usually a black animal. We're all so original
MIDRIFF	Greyhounds
MIGHTY JOE YOUNG	Any of the big, heavy breeds . . . Newfoundlands, Saint Bernards, Bernese mountain dogs
MIKADO	An operetta lover's pet
MIKIMOTO	The best pearl store in the jewelry district
MIKKI	Chinese crested dogs
MILANO	Either you like the city in Italy, or the cookie in America
MILDRED	Redbone coonhounds . . . wonderful name
MILDRED PIERCE	You loved Joan Crawford
MILFORD	A pet from Connecticut
MILICENT	Millie's proper name
MILKMAN	Always the one who gets the blame
MILLARD	For a pet that's never full . . . always wants to fill more
MILLER	Iceland dogs
MILLIE	Was in the same bunk with me and Mimi (see Mimi)
MILLSTONE	Your pet is a burden
MILO	Famous Greek athlete

MILQUETOAST	Your pet is a wuss
MILTON	Gordon setters . . . I happen to know Milton Gordon. So, I like it
MILTON BERLE	Your pet has a very racy comedy act
MILWAUKEE BRAVE	You're a Milwaukee Brave fan
MIMI	The only girl I ever met who knew how to be sexy at eleven years old
MIMMI	Chow Chows, tabbies
MIMOSA	A type of tree and a type of drink
MIMSY	Your pet gets involved in town gossip
MINERVA	A Manx . . . nice name for a cat
MINESTRONE	Italian hounds
MING	For the breeding pet that you expect to start a dynasty
MINIKIN	A darling . . . anything small and rare
MINNA	Yorkies, silkies, Chihuahuas
MINNESOTA FATS	Jackie Gleason as a basset hound
MINNIE	Mickey Mouse's girlfriend
MINNOW	Any of the water dogs . . . Irish, Portuguese . . . or, any of the retrievers
MINSKOFF	You're in the theater
MINT JULEP	American (Southern) longhaired tabbies
MINUET	A pet that takes small, tiny dance steps
MINUTE MOUSE	For the gerbil, mouse, or hamster that you don't expect to last too long
MINUTEMAN	A pet that doesn't dawdle when you take it out
MIRABELLA	Your pet is into magazines
MIRABELLE	European plum tree (that's a tree . . . not another animal with a strange name)
MIRANDA	For a pet not sure of its sexuality
MIRÓ	A painter's pet
MISHA	A ballet dancer's pet

MISS AMERICA	American pit bull terrier . . . no chauvinism here!
MISS BROOKS	A pet you can call 'Our'
MISS DAISY	It likes to be driven
MISS KITTY	Any adorable kitten . . . who has a sheriff for a boyfriend
MISS LONELYHEARTS	Neutered pets
MISS MARPLE	You love the books
MISS MONEYPENNY	Pair with James Bond
MISS MUFFET	For any pet that has its own tuffet
MISS PIGGY	For a pig or a pet that overeats
MISS PRIGGY	Ridiculous
MISS PURRFECT	Also ridiculous, however, there are cats out there with that name
MISS VICKY	For a pet that likes to tiptoe through the tulips
MISSHIE	Maine coons
MISSIE	My ex-husband's cat
MISSILE	For a hyperactive pet
MISSION IMPOSSIBLE	For the absolutely untrainable pet
MISSONI	A designer's pet
MISTER	A former knight's pet
MISTI	See Misty
MISTLETOE	For a very affectionate pet
MISTRAL	Poet, Frederic. Also, a strong wind in Provence. So, a poetic pet with gas
MISTY	A weatherman's pet
MITCH	American foxhounds . . . sweet and affectionate, and hard workers
MITCHELL	Good name . . . and, you use the hair products
MITTENS	For any pet that has different color paws
MIZRAHI	A designer's pet
MOBY DICK	For the biggest fish in the tank

MOCHA	Any of the mocha-colored pets
MODIGLIANI	Artist
MOE	Triple with Larry and Curly
MOHAWK	You periodically shave your pet
MOHICAN	For the last of your pets
MOLAR	A dentist's pet
MOLASSES	For very slow pets
MOLIÈRE	A playwright's pet
MOLLY	One of the more popular names
MOLLY MAGUIRE	For an Irish-American guard dog
MOLOTOV	Your pet enjoys cocktails
MOMBASA	Salukis, Rhodesian ridgebacks
MONA	For a pet with a wry smile
MONACO	Royal Standards, King Charles spaniels
MONEYPENNY	A pet for someone named James
MONICA	Sphinx creams, fish, parrots
MONIQUE	French pointers, French poodles, French bulldogs
MONOGRAM	For a person whose name is initials, like BJ or JB
MONROE	Wirehaired pointing griffons
MONTANA	Very cool, western, laid-back name
MONTE CARLO	A gambler's pet
MONTE CRISTO	You're a Count
MONTESQUIEU	Another regal pet name
MONTGOMERY	For a pet that will live on a cliff (t)
MONTY	Good name, and actually, my friend Monty is responsible for my present beau (I hate to say "boyfriend")
MOOCH	A freeloader's pet
MOODY	Either a Moody Blues fan . . . or a pet with PMS
MOOKIE	Too cutesie. Although I like Pookie. Go figure
MOOLAH	You think about money a lot
MOON	For a pet with a big face

MOON QUEEN	Just one of those names . . . if you like it—use it
MOONDOGGIE	Gidget's boyfriend. A surfer's pet
MOONSTALK	Another one
MOOSE	Either for a Yorkie or a Kuvasz (huge . . . 110 lbs.)
MORDECHAI	For religious pets
MORGAN	Your pet will wear a belt
MORNING GLORY	An early riser's pet
MORNING STAR	Another choice
MOROCCO	Exotic pets
MORRIS	A name made famous by the cat food commercial
MORSE CODE	Your pet, miraculously, knows how to communicate with you
MORTICIA	Great name for a mortician to give his pet
MORTIMER	Giant schnauzers, Old English sheepdogs, Himalayans
MORTON	For an old, salty dog
MOSAIC	For a pet of many colors
MOSCOW	Borzois, Russian wolfhounds. There is also a breed called Moscow
MOTHER GOOSE	For any breeding animal
MOTOROLA	You love your car phone more than any other recent invention
MOUSER	A mouse chaser's name
MOVADO	Your pet tells time
MOVER	A good name for a Hamster that has a running wheel in its cage
MOXIE	A pushy person's pet
MOZART	A music aficionado's pet
MR. BECKS	A beer lover's pet
MR. BLUE	A depressive's pet
MR. CLEAN	For a pet with an earring
MR. DEEDS	For a pet that goes to town

MR. DOOLEY	For a pet who hangs down his head
MR. MAGOO	Pugs
MR. MEPHISTOPHELES	Cats
MR. PEEPERS	Pugs, bulldogs, sheepdogs
MR. PRESIDENT	It has a large ego
MR. PURRFECT	See Miss Purrfect
MR. ROBERTS	A sailor's pet
MR. ROGERS	For a neutered pet
MR. SMITH	It will go to Washington
MR. T	A bejeweled rough-coated Bohemian pointer
MRS. COLUMBO	For a female version of the scruffy Columbo
MRS. FLETCHER	You like mysteries
MRS. HOWELL	You're a Gilligan fan
MRS. MINIVER	The charming movie from the '50s
MRS. POLIFAX	Wonderful older woman who spies for the CIA
MUCH ADO	Your pet has a flourish
MUELLER	German hunting terriers, German hounds
MUFFIE	Muffie reminds me of fluffy, so I would use this for a ragdoll or Persian
MUFFIN	A WASP's pet
MUFFLES	A hard-of-hearing person's pet
MUGGS	Mixed breeds
MUHAMMAD ALI	The great Cassius Clay. It would have to be a boxer
MULDOON	Toody's partner . . . *Car 54, Where Are You?*
MULLIGAN STEW	Mixed breeds
MUMBLES	Good name for a parrot
MUMMY	A rap person's pet. (Get it? Wrapped? *The Mummy?*)

MUMPS	Pugs, bulldogs
MUPPET	Your pet looks like a puppet
MURIEL	Another perfect animal name
MURPHY	Irish wolfhounds, Irish setters, Irish terriers, etc.
MURPHY BROWN	A reporter's pet
MURRAY	Outstanding name for any animal
MUSCLES	Boxers
MUSHROOM	For the pet that will get much bigger than you originally thought
MUSTARD	Golden Persians
MUTZIE	An endearing name
MUU MUU	A fat person's pet
MY FRIEND FLICKA	You have a horse
MY MAN GODFREY	Great movie, and Godfrey is a wonderful pet name
MYLAR	Silver pointed tabbies
MYTH	Perfect for someone with a lithp
MYTHTER	Also

NABBER	For a mouser
NABOKOV	Vladimir
NABOR	For your neighbor, named Jim
NADER	Activist pet—demands constant consumer protection
NAGGER	It doesn't stop whining till you feed it
NAMATH	A pet from Broadway
NAMELESS	When, try as you might, you just can't come up with a name
NAMO	One of Charlemagne's knights
NANA	The Newfoundland from *Peter Pan*
NANCY	I can't imagine a cuter name for a pet
NANCY DREW	A pet of mysterious parentage
NANNY	Another one for the Newfoundland
NANTERS	Myth. British king
NANTES	Myth. Site of Caradoc's castle
NANTUCKET	A pet you have to get to by ferry
NAPA	A Valley pet
NAPE	Myth. One of the dogs pursuing Actaeon when Diana changed him into a stag

NAPOLEON	Yorkies
NARCISSUS	Myth. Son of Cephisus
NARNIA	Cavalier King Charles spaniels, turtles, macaws
NARRATOR	Another good parrot name
NASH	For an Ogden
NASHUA	A pet from a New Hampshire industrial town
NASHVILLE	You love country western
NASSER	A pet for a high-ranking Egyptian official
NASSIM	A Russian name
NASTASE	It may be Russian, but it's definitely tennis
NAT	Seems like a very chummy name for your pet
NATALIE	I don't want to say woodpecker
NATASHA	Russian wolfhounds, Moscows, Siberian huskies . . . pair with Boris
NATE	Al's partner in the L.A. Deli
NATIONAL	An aspiring Budget rental agent's pet
NATIONAL VELVET	Elizabeth Taylor's horse story
NATIVE SON	An all-American pet
NATURAL	Pulis
NATWICK	A pet for a Mildred
NAUSICAA	From Homer . . . daughter of Alcinous
NAUSITHOUS	Myth. King of the Phaeacians
NAVAJO	See Native Son
NAVARRO	Prefers to go by airplane instead
NAVEL	You're fascinated by belly buttons
NAVRATILOVA	Tennis is your game
NAVY	A sailor's pet
NAXOS	Myth. Largest island of the Cyclades group in the Aegean Sea
NBC	Triple with CBS and ABC

NEAL	My next-door neighbor, who had a three-legged dog . . . Taffy
NEBUCHADNEZZAR	A mean, Old Testament king
NECK	Bulldogs, boxers
NECTAR	Celestial beverage of the gods
NED	A Beatty pet
NEELIA	*Valley of the Dolls*
NEESON	Scottish terriers, or is it Welch corgis?
NEGOTIATOR	For the pet that makes peace in the family
NEGRI	Black pets
NEGUS	An Amharic word meaning 'king'
NEHRU	For an Indian cat
NEIL	See Neal, I'm actually not sure how he spelled his name
NEIMAN	A shopper's pet
NELLI	My friend Ina's King Charles spaniel
NELLY	This ranks right up there with Molly for great pet names
NELLYBELLE	Roy Rogers's jeep
NELSON	For *Ozzie and Harriet* fans
NEMEA	Myth. Nemean games were held in honor of Jupiter and Hercules
NEMESIS	Myth. Goddess of just distribution
NENNI	Seal bicolor ragdolls, frogs, fish
NEON	Flashy pets
NEOPTOLEMUS	Son of Achilles
NEOSHO	Japanese beetles, Japanese spitzes
NEPENTHE	Myth. Egyptian drug fabled to drive away cares and woes
NEPHELE	Myth. Mother of Phyrius and Helle
NEPHTHYS	Myth. Egyptian goddess
NEPTUNE	For one of the larger fish in the tank
NEREIDS	Myth. Sea Nymphs . . . daughters of Nereus and Doris

NEREUS	Myth. Father of the water nymphs . . . for any pet that loves to swim
NERO	Fiddle-playing pets
NESBITT	A pet for a Cathleen
NESSUS	Myth. Centaur killed by Hercules
NESTOR	Myth. King of Pylos, renowned for his wisdom
NETTLA	A character from *Bambi*
NETWORK	An aspiring cable executive's pet
NEURON	Very small pets
NEVADA	A quickie divorced person's pet
NEVIL	Gordon setters . . . Scottish ancestry . . . intelligent and pleasant
NEW JERSEY	You've moved and miss it
NEW YEAR'S	Very festive pets
NEWBURY	You like Boston
NEWLEY	For an Anthony
NEWMAN	For a Paul
NEWPORT	For a Californian
NEWS ITEM	For a parrot
NEWSWEEK	For a pet that likes to keep on top of current events
NEWTON	For a pet that likes Juice
NEXT	For the second of the litter
NFL	A Sunday football widow's pet
NIAD	Myth. A nymph of a lake, river, etc.
NIAGARA	Pets partial to wearing highly starched collars
NIBBLER	Gerbils, rabbits
NIBELUNG	Myth. Originally a race of dwarfs
NICCOLO	That commercial drives me crazy . . . but, if YOU want to keep yelling "N i c c o l o !" go ahead
NICHOLAS	Good name. My friend Andrea's Jack Russell terrier up in New Hampshire is Nicholas

NICHOLAS NICKELBY	Perfect for a Dickens fan
NICHOLE	Longhaired chestnut Angoras
NICHOLETTE	Little French poodles, Yorkies, Maltese
NICHOLS	For someone that likes to shop in London
NICK	Asta's pet (see Nora)
NICK AT NIGHT	Outdoor guard dogs
NICK CHARLES	Nora Charles's husband in *The Thin Man* series
NICKELODEON	Your family is into TV
NICKIE	What Nora called Nick in *The Thin Man* series
NICKS	You're a hockey fan
NICOLAI	Russian breeds
NICOLETTE	French bulldogs, French mastiffs
NIDIA	Not quite a Lidia
NIETZSCHE	Very philosophical pets
NIFLHEIM	Myth. One of the nine worlds
NIFTY	A cool pet
NIGEL	Great! Giant schnauzers, Saint Bernards, Great Danes, etc.
NIGGS	Teeny-weeny silky terriers, hamsters, lizards
NIGHT	Any black animal
NIGHTINGALE	A nurse's pet
NIJINSKY	A dancer's pet
NIKE	Greyhounds
NIKITA	Russian borzois, Balkan hounds, Magyar Agars
NIKKI	The borzoi's nickname
NILE	For a river animal . . . snakes, lizards, frogs
NILES	You like Frasier's brother
NIM	Kim's brother
NIMBUS	A cloudy pet

NIMITZ	Black-and-white smoke Devon rexes
NIMOY	Your pet has pointy ears
NIMROD	A mighty hunter . . . grandson of Noah and son of Ham
NIN	For an Anaïs
NINA	My dear cousin in Boston . . . triple with Pinta and Santa Maria
NINE	Daring cats
NINETY-NINE	Pair with Maxwell Smart
NINI	Italian pointers, Italian greyhounds, Italian hounds
NINNIUS	Myth. Brother of Cassibellaun, conquered by Caesar
NINO	Volpino Italianos . . . this dog stays under nine pounds
NINTENDO	For a pet that keeps your kids company for hours at the TV
NINUS	Myth. Son of Belus . . . reputed builder of Nineveh
NIOBE	Myth. Daughter of Tantalus, queen of Thebes
NIPPER	The little nipper. (Better than a Big nipper)
NISUS	Myth. A king of Megara . . . he was changed to an eagle
NITA	A very clean pet
NITDHOGG	Myth. A serpent . . . so, there's a good one for snakes
NITTY	Small pets
NIVEN	David's pet
NIVIE	Smooth fox terriers
NIVINS	Sounds like a butler
NIXON	Too smart for its own good
NOAH	An ark builder's pet
NOAM	Miniature Alaskan huskies (Malamute)

NOBEL	Show dogs that usually win the blue ribbon
NOBLEMAN	Spanish mastiffs, French mastiffs, Great Danes
NOEL	It was born on Christmas day
NOGUCHI	A sculptor's pet
NOISE	For a pet that won't stop talking, barking, mewing, or whatever
NOLTE	For a Nick fan
NOMAD	Alley cats
NONCHALANT	For a very mellow and casual pet
NONPARTISAN	An independent's pet
NOODLES	My friends Vivien and Bob's cairn terrier
NORA	A solid, reliable pet
NORA CHARLES	Nick Charles's wife in *The Thin Man* series
NORBERT	Nor Ernie, either
NORBIE	Bichon frises, gerbils, guinea pigs
NOREEN	Irish setters, Irish wolfhounds, Irish terriers, etc.
NOREL	Australian silky terriers
NORELL	You love the perfume
NORMA	My aunt . . . the mother of Doris, Maggie, Paulette, Dina, and Frank . . . wife of Sam
NORMAN	*Cheers* anyone?
NORRIS	Chuck anyone?
NORSEMAN	Norwegian elkhounds
NORTH	This one's for Ollie
NORTH POLE	Siberian huskies, Eskimo dogs
NORTON	Pair with Kramden
NORVELL	Border terriers
NORWAY	Norwegian elkhounds
NORWOOD	American foxhounds
NOSTALGIA	A cat on its ninth life—wants to be back in one of the previous eight

NOSTRADAMUS	For a stargazer
NOTEWORTHY	For a pet that one notices
NOTHUNG	Myth. A magic sword
NOTORIOUS	You're a Hitchcock fan
NOTUS	Myth. Personification of the south wind . . . good for a bird
NOVA SCOTIA	For your not-too-salty fish
NOVAK	For a Kim or a Siamese
NOVELLA	An author's pet
NOVEMBER	You got it in November
NOW	A feminist's pet . . . National Organization for Women
NOX	Myth. A goddess
NOXZEMA	For a very clean pet with good skin
NUFFI	Newfoundlands
NUGENT	A high school coach in the '60s
NUKE	Bionic dogs
NUMA POMPILIUS	Legendary second king of Rome
NUMBERS	A gambler's pet
NUNZIE	Ruddy wild Abyssinians
NUNZIO	Italian greyhounds, Turkish vans
NUPTIAL	It was a wedding gift
NUREYEV	A dancer's pet
NURSE	White animals
NURSE RATCHET	A nasty ol' cat ready to fly over the cuckoo's nest
NUTMEG	A pet named Meg—a little out to lunch
NYET	Needs obedience school
NYMPH	For one or your smaller breeds
NYMPHETTE	For an even smaller breed, light on its feet

NYNEX   When your phone bill is consistently
                   higher than your mortgage

**THE NEW
YORKER**   For a pet from New York, living
                   elsewhere

O'BRIEN	Irish wolfhounds
O'CASEY	Irish setters
O'CONNOR	For an *All in the Family* fan
O'HARA	A Scarlett pet or a Southern one
O'KEEFE	Irish water spaniels
O'KEEFFE	Either you're from Georgia or you're into strange-looking flowers
O'LEARY	An Irish pet that's a bit on the cautious side
O'NEILL	For a pet in the theater
O'REE	Irish blue terriers
O'RORKE	You already have a Mickey
O'RYAN	A movie lover's pet
O'SHEA	Irish terriers
O'SULLIVAN	For pets with famous daughters
O'TOOLE	A Peter fan
O.J.	I guess this is a no-no right now
OAKIE	Remember 'Oakie Fanoakie'? It's a cute name if you think about it
OAKLAND	A pet from California

OAKLEY	An Annie fan
OASIS	A pet from the desert
OATCAKE	You're on a diet
OATES	Great name. Sounds just right when you say it
OATH	A judge's pet
OATIE	Oatmeal's nickname
OATMEAL	You love a hearty breakfast
OATS	Silky terriers . . . lively and cheerful . . . can really feel their oats
OATSUNG	The actual pronunciation of Oudtshoorn
OBERARTH	A small Swiss village
OBERRUNON	Also a small Swiss village . . . where I lived for one month . . . too long
OBERTH	Brood mares
OBI	Wan Kenobi . . . your pet is gentle and wise
OBIE	Bloodhounds . . . wonderful sense of smell, timid, and good-natured
OBLONG	Wirehair dachshunds
OCEAN	Fish
OCEANUS	Myth. A Titan ruling the watery elements
OCTOBER	It was born in October
OCTOBER FEST	It loves beer
OCYRRHOE	Myth. A prophetess
ODALIS	Basset griffon vendeens . . . small, but courageous and tenacious
ODDJOB	A pet that can toss a hat and make an impact
ODELIA	King Charles spaniels
ODERIC	Myth. The false night
ODESSA	For someone who likes filing
ODET	You lament how much you spent on it
ODETTA	It's become your mantra

ODIE	Great Swiss mountain dogs . . . loyal, courageous, and wise
ODIN	Myth. God of wisdom
ODYAR	A famous Frankis hero
ODYSSEUS	Borzois
ODYSSEY	Homer's poem
ODYSSIA	Bronze Egyptian Maus
ODZANENDS	Mutts
OEDIPUP	A puppy with an Oedipal complex
OEDIPUS REX	The king of all Oedipal complexes
OEDIPUSS	A kitty with an Oedipal complex
OENEUS	Myth. A king of Calydon
OENONE	Myth. A nymph married by Paris in his youth
OENOPION	Myth. King of Chios
OETA	Myth. Scene of Hercules' death
OFFBEAT	A pet without an Oedipal complex
OFFICER	Guard dogs
OGDEN	You like to read
OGIER THE DANE	One of the great heroes of medieval romance
OHIO	Japanese spitz
OHRBACH	For a nostalgic shopper
OKALOOSA	Sounds like a basset hound
OKEMO	Rhodesian ridgebacks
OLAF	Bosnian hounds, border collies
OLAJUWON	Hakeem The Dream
OLD ENGLISH	A great aftershave . . . your pet smells good
OLD FAITHFUL	Good for a Labrador . . . reminds me of Old Yeller
OLD MAID	For a female that's never had a litter
OLD MAN	For a male that's too old to have a litter
OLD MAN AND THE SEA	Old Portuguese water dogs

OLD YELLER	Yellow Labs
OLEANDER	Golden Persians
OLÉ	Bulls
OLIVE OYL	You are either a Popeye fan or a salad lover
OLIVER	For a pet with a love story
OLIVER TWIST	A pet you rescue from the pound
OLIVIA	An actor's pet
OLIVIER	Also an actor's pet
OLLIE	Also an actor's pet
OLLY	Triple with Kookla and Fran
OLSEN	Lois Lane's coworker, Jimmy
OLWEN	Myth. Wife of Kilwich
OLYMPIA	Myth. A valley in Elis, celebrated for the sanctuary of Zeus
OLYMPIAN	Harlequin Great Danes
OLYMPIAN ZEUS	Tawny Great Danes
OLYMPUS	Dwelling place of the dynasty of gods
OMAR	Egyptian Sphinx, Salukis
OMAR KHAYYÁM	Eleventh-century Persian poet
OMBUDSMAN	For the pet that you appoint to investigate complaints within the family
OMEGA	A watcher
OMELET	French mastiffs, French bulldogs, poodles, etc.
OMPHALE	Myth. Queen of Lydia to whom Hercules was bound as a slave. He then fell in love with her
ONASSIS	Very rich Greek hounds
ONCE	For a pet that listens and obeys the first time
ONDREI	Small Continental spaniels
ONEIDA	You're into silverware
ONION	Your pet has a lot of layers

ONO	For a naughty pet
ONOMATOPOEIA	A pet with good grammar
ONYX	Black smoke American shorthairs
OODLES OF NOODLES	Pulis
OOH	Bullterriers
OOPLA	Your pet loves being thrown up in the air. And caught, of course
OPAL	Blue-Cream point Himalayans
OPAQUE	For a pet that you can't see through
OPERA	You love operas
OPERATOR	The neighborhood gossip
OPEY	You watch *The Andy Griffith Show* reruns
OPHELIA	Afghans, Angoras
OPHION	Myth. The king of the Titans
OPIE	*The Andy Griffith Show,* again
OPPENHEIMER	A pet that's into investing
OPRAH	It will, one day, have its own talk show, lose weight, and look marvelous!
OPTION	A stock broker's pet
OPUS	A great work of writing or music
ORANGE	Orange tabbies
ORANGE BLOSSOM	Red shorthaired Asians, red setters, Pomeranians
ORANGE JULIUS	Oriental reds
ORANGEADE	Red spotted British shorthairs
ORANTES	Athletic pets
ORBIS	Fish
ORBIT	Birds
ORC	Myth. A sea monster that devoured men and women
ORCHID	A very delicate pet that needs constant room temperature
OREAD	Myth. A mountain or hill nymph

OREGANO	Italian hounds
OREO	For a black-and-white anything
ORESTES	Myth. Son of Agamemnon and Clytemnestra
ORGANDY	For a beautiful, fluffy, willowy cat
ORGANZA	For a rather more stiff but still feminine cat
ORIGINAL SIN	Snakes
ORIOLE	Fancy Manhattan restaurant
ORION	Myth. A giant and hunter, son of Neptune
ORITHYIA	Myth. A nymph
ORLANDO	You love to be reminded of Disney World
ORLANDO II	Nephew of Charlemagne, celebrated knight
ORLOFF	Black smoke and white Scottish folds
ORMANDY	A conductor's pet
ORMAZD	Destined to prevail over evil
ORNAMENT	What my friend told her husband she was when he asked her to get a job
ORNATE	For an ultrafancy pet
OROONOKO	I have no idea where I got this . . . or how to pronounce it
ORPHA	Dandie Dinmont terriers, turtles, rabbits
ORPHEE	Akitas, Airedales
ORPHEUS	Myth. Son of Apollo and Calliope
ORTEGA	Spanish mastiffs . . . big, robust guard dogs, but vivacious and affectionate
ORTHODOX	For a religious pet
ORVIS	For an athletic pet
ORWELL	For a pet born in 1984
ORZO	For a pasta loving pet
OSBORNE	For an American foxhound
OSCAR	For a pet that loves trash

OSCAR ROBERTSON	The Big O
OSGOOD	For a pet into bow ties
OSHKOSH	For a pet into overalls
OSHA	Government pets
OSIRIS	One of the chief gods of Egyptian mythology
OSKAR	German shepherds
OSLO	Swedish elkhounds
OSMOND	For a Donny or Marie
OSMOSIS	For a pet that does your bidding without your saying a word
OSSA	Myth. Mountain in Thessaly
OSSI	Ossicats
OSSIAN	Legendary Gaelic bard and warrior of the third century
OSSIP	For someone who's not quite a gossip
OSTENTATIOUS	Flashy pets
OSWALD	People will immediately be leery of it
OTHELLO	For Shakespeare buffs
OTIS	Wonderful pet name. Appropriate for almost any type of animal or breed
OTIS REDDING	Your pet likes to sit in the mornin' sun
OTTO	This is also one of those universal endearing names
OUDTSHOORN	A town in South Africa where they breed ostriches
OUNCE	For your smaller breeds
OUTDO	Your pet is going to be wearing great collars
OUTIE	Innie's brother
OUTLAW	Any pet that has dark rings around both eyes
OUTLET	A shopper's pet
OUTRAGEOUS	Not for a meek pet
OUTSIDER	For an outdoor pet

OUTTAKE	A TV producer's pet
OVID	Latin poet in the time of Augustus
OWAIN	A knight of King Arthur's court
OWEN	Marshall . . . counselor at law
OWNER	Who's the boss?
OXFORD	For someone into good sheets or good schools
OZ	For a wizard
OZANNA	A knight of King Arthur's Round Table
OZAWA	Rhodesian ridgebacks
OZER	For a funny-looking pet
OZONE	For a pet with his head in the clouds
OZZIE	Harriet, Ricky, and David . . . the Nelson family

PABLO Any of the Spanish breeds . . . Spanish mastiff, Spanish greyhound, etc.

PACKER A pet that's always threatening to leave

PADDY Irish wolfhounds, Irish setters, Irish water dogs

PAHLAVI Where caviar is harvested . . . for someone in your fish tank

PAIGE A 1950s WASPish name that doesn't seem to be so popular any more

PAISLEY A pet with a lot of colors—American wirehair tortoiseshell and white, for instance

PALADIN The wonderful gunslinging cowboy from the '60s TV show that my grandmother loved

PALERMO A Sicilian pet

PALM BEACH Sunny and rich. An Afghan would be gorgeous

PALOMA Your pet used to be 'X', now you want it to have a proper name

PAM Was a cheerleader with me in school

PAMELA	Her given name
PANACEA	You can't believe it's so perfect
PANACHE	A pet with style and flare
PANAMA	A pet into hats
PANDORA	A pet constantly coming up with unpleasant surprises
PANSY	Triple with Rose and Violet
PAOLO	Portuguese water dogs, Spanish mastiffs, Chihuahuas
PAPA	It's a pedigree and you plan to breed him for a long time
PAR	A golfer's pet
PARADISE	An American pet that is just perfect in every way
PARADISO	An Italian pet that is just perfect in every way
PARALLAX	A pet that gives you a different view
PARIS	It was the last time you saw it
PARKAY	When it looks so good . . . you can't believe that it's not pedigree
PARKER	You love pens
PARKWAY	You don't live near a highway or a freeway
PARMESAN	Not what I would call a cheesy name
PARSLEY	The green vegetable that is good for bad breath
PARTNER	A pet you will take to work with you
PARTRIDGE	It came from a large family
PARTY GIRL	Any outgoing female
PARVIS	Part this, and part that
PASCAL	Bedlington terriers (they look like lambs)
PASHA	For any of the royal breeds . . . King Charles spaniel, Royal Standard poodle, etc.
PASSION	Great for a pit bull

PASTA	You love the food enough to be constantly reminded of it
PASTERNAK	For a *Dr. Zhivago* fan
PASTEUR	A dairyman's pet
PATCHWORK	Multicolored pets
PATEK	Any of the French breeds
PATEK PHILIPPE	Any of the French breeds that are sensitive to time
PATHFINDER	Any of the hunting breeds
PATRICK	A man that used to say the most outlandish things to me in the early '70s at Holt, Rinehart & Winston. And, if you're reading this, Patrick, I liked it. Where are you now?
PATRICK HENRY	For any of the Irish breeds that were born in America
PATRIOT	Your pet stands at attention when the national anthem is played
PATSY	Your pet always takes the blame
PATTON	For the pet that should take the blame
PAUL BUNYAN	Either for your giant breeds . . . or pets with problem feet
PAVAROTTI	A pet with huge lungs
PAVE	You're in the diamond business
PAVLOV	You think he's trained, but YOU'RE the one going out as soon as you wake up
PAVLOVA	Russian ballerina . . . borzois . . . tall and graceful
PAWS	Nice name for a cat with different color paws
PAX	For a peaceful pet
PAYOLA	Perfect if you were a disc jockey in the '60s
PEA SHOOTER	Good for rabbits
PEABODY	English bulldogs, English foxhounds, English setters

PEACHES	Pair with Cream
PEANUT	For any of your toy breeds
PEANUT BUTTER	Pair with Jelly . . . by the way, good to use for getting chewing gum out of hair. I don't know about fur
PEAR	A fruit lover's pet
PEARL	For any of your minis
PEAT	A gardener's pet
PEBBLES	Pair with Bamm Bamm
PECK	You have a very affectionate pet . . . or a bird that keeps jabbing you
PEDRO	My tile man . . . who drives a Mercedes
PEEPERS	Old English sheepdogs
PEEWEE	Any small pet . . . mice, hamsters, minis, parakeets
PEEWEE REISS	You like marbles
PEGASUS	Finally, a name for a horse! Hopefully, it didn't spring from Medusa's body upon her death
PEGGY	For an honest-to-goodness, easygoing, reliable pet
PÉLÉ	Your pet is good with its feet
PENDLETON	Briards, bearded collies, brindle Great Danes
PENELOPE	A pet that costs more than a Penny does
PENN	An ex-con's pet
PENNE	An Italian ex-con's pet
PENNY	It cost less than Penelope
PENROD	Wirehaired dachshunds
PEONY	Wonderful in an arrangement with Blossom, Violet, Daisy and Daffodil
PEORIA	Your pet came from Illinois
PEPA	Pair with Salt
PEPPER	Pair with Salt (and, that's it for Pepper pairs)

PEPPERMINT	For your fresh-smelling pet
PEPPERONI	For your spotted pets
PEPPY	What a name for a basset hound
PEPSI	Pair with Coke
PERCY	A pet that keeps going into your handbag
PERIWINKLE	A snail or mussel . . . or any of your blue breeds
PERKINS	You really wanted a butler but settled for the pet
PERÓN	Dictatorial pets
PEROT	Your pet wants to run for office
PEROXIDE	A blonde's pet
PERRY	Great for Perry Mason fans . . . pair with Della
PERSIA	A Persian . . . what else?
PERSNICKETY	For a fastidious, fussy pet
PESKY	The original name for mosquitoes
PESTO	Gooey, green sauce, full of garlic. Skunks, turtles, frogs, garden snakes
PETE	Good, solid work dog
PETER	Pete's formal name
PETER PAN	Your pet refuses to grow up
PETER PIPER	Your pet manages to attract all the animals in the neighborhood
PETITFOUR	For a yummy, many layered, multifaceted cat
PETRA	My cousin's roommate when she lived in New York City
PETTIBONES	One of the Lawrence Sanders characters in the *McNally* series
PETUNIA	Yet another flower
PHANTOM	Good name for a disappearing cat
PHARAOH	Pharaoh dogs. That was easy

PHI BETA KAPPA	You didn't make it, but you hope your pet will make up for it
PHILADELPHIA STORY	For a Grace Kelly fan
PHILIE	A whipped Philip
PHILIP	A queen's Philip
PHILIP MORRIS	A smoker's Philip
PHILIPPA	French female Philip
PHILIPPE	French male Philip
PHLAPPJACK	Bassett hounds
PHLASH	He's very fast
PHOEBE	Another of the great pet names . . . good for any type of female
PHOENICIA	Exotic, longhaired pets
PHOENIX	For any pet that rises again and again
PHONOGRAPH	For those who remember the days before tapes, CDs, CD ROMs, videos, audios, stereo, and surround sound
PHYLLIS	Your pet intends to be queen of comedy, piano, and plastic surgery
PIA	Another pet that has questionable control skills
PIAF	For aficionados of cabaret singers
PIANO	A mitted tabby that walks the piano keys
PICA	For a very small breed, reminiscent of small print
PICASSO	An artist's pet
PICAYUNE	An accountant's pet
PICCADILLY	For those who love London
PICCOLO	It means 'small' in Italian
PICKETT	For sign-carrying pets or Wilson fans
PICKLES	Snakes, frogs, turtles
PICKWICK	For a pet that goes on papers
PIED PIPER	A pet in heat

PIELS	A beer lover's pet
PIERRE	How very French, my dear
PIKE	For a very tall breed, reminiscent of Pike's Peak
PILAR	A pet from India
PILOT	I know there's a type of dog featured with goggles on, behind the wheel of a plane
PIM	Abyssinian blues, silver spotted British shorthairs or California spangleds
PINK LADY	I remember having this drink in school . . . but, I don't remember what it was
PINK PANTHER	Your pet constantly sneaks up on you
PINKERTON	For any of the English detective-type breeds
PINKNEY	My vet. And, a good name too
PINKY	Rabbits
PINK LEE	Television star, show of the same name 1961. You-hoo it's me
PINOCCHIO	Any pet with a long snout . . . a dachshund would be perfect . . . borzois
PINTO BEAN	A Chihuahua (I will NEVER learn to spell this without looking it up)
PIONEER	You're in the electronics business
PIP	For a pet that can take a joke
PIPER	Piper Laurie
PIPER-HEIDSIECK	You will be doing most of your celebrating with your pet
PIPPI	Pippi Longstocking
PIPPIN	They named a Broadway show after it
PIPSQUEAK	Pip's full name
PIRATE	Any pet that steals your food or clothing
PI SQUARE	A mathematician's pet
PISSARRO	Camille . . . impressionist
PISTACHIO	So good, but so much work

PITA	Kangaroos
PITTER	Patter's pair
PIXIE	Either petite pets or vicious big ones
PIZARRO	Francisco. Spanish conqueror of Peru (1475–1541)
PIZZA	A restaurateur's pet
PIZZAZZ	Your pet has real style and charm
PJ	A cat that loves to sleep
PLACEBO	For people who have bought a pet because they are not ready to have kids yet
PLANET HOLLYWOOD	Your pet loves the limelight
PLASTIC	For *The Graduate*
PLATH	For a depressed pet
PLATO	A very studious pet . . . or a pet that knows when to retreat
PLATOON	English bulldogs, boxers, pugs
PLAYBOY	Un-neutered males
PLAYER	A Jack Russell terrier that keeps bringing the damn ball back over and over and over and over
PLAZA	Ivana Trump's former pet
PLUM	You got the pick of the litter
PLUTO	Disney cartoon character
PMS	You ended up with the moodiest animal you've ever owned
POACHER	Any animal that likes to steal food
POE	As in Edgar Allan . . . your pet has a dark side
POET	Any pet that looks studious
POGO	Reminds me of Dandie Dinmont terriers
POINSETTIA	Any showy animal
POINTER	Not very original, but a good name for a German shorthaired pointer
POLAR STAR	An outdoor pet

POLARIS	The North Star . . . or . . . the US ballistic missile with nuclear warhead. So . . . either a sweet and cuddly or a lunatic
POLICY	A Congressman's pet
POLIFAX	For those into the Mrs. Polifax mysteries
POLLY	I know 'Polly Wanna Cracker' is pushing it . . . but, this isn't so easy!
POLO	For a Ralph or a Marco
POLYGAMIST	A stud animal
POM-POM	Your pet looks like a cheerleader
POMPIDOU	French bulldogs
PONCE DE LEÓN	You live in Florida and believe that this pet is the answer
PONCHO	Great for Chihuahuas, Spanish mastiffs
POO BEAR	From Winnie the Poo
POOCHIE	A doggie designer
POOCHINNI	A doggie composer
POODIE	For a peekaboo (poodle & Pekingese combination)
POOF	What happens to Puddles if he doesn't shape up quickly! (See Puddles)
POOH BAH	From Gilbert & Sullivan's *The Mikado*
POOR RICHARD	For the cat you get while still owning three dogs
POPCORN	Great for a bichon
POPPER	Japanese bobtails, rabbits, frogs
POPPY	For the stud animal
PORGY	Pair with Bess
PORSCHE	One day I will get this. A 1957 would make me so happy, not to mention so poor
PORT	A lovely liquor that's a bit heavy
PORTABLE	Any pet easy to carry with you
PORTER	A pet either good with luggage, or good with music
PORTFOLIO	An investment banker's pet

PORTIA	The heroine in Shakespeare's *Merchant of Venice*
PORTNOY	Your pet never stops complaining
PORTOBELLO	You love the mushrooms
POSHA	A rich Arab's pet
POSTCARD	A traveler's pet
POSTMAN	When you're not sure who the father was
POT	Pair with Pan
POTLUCK	What you see is what you get
POTPIE	Turtles
POTTER	Colonel Potter from *M*A*S*H**
POTTS	Different from Pots and Pans . . . an English pet, perhaps
POUNCE	A cat that loves to scare you
POWDER	Possibility for those interested in the white stuff . . . skiers, I mean
PRADA	For a very expensive pet of Italian heritage
PRANCER	If you have a reindeer . . . perfection
PREAKNESS	For a racing aficionado
PRECIOUS	I think it's usually a nickname
PREDATOR	Good name for either a Doberman or a Yorkie
PREEMIE	Perfect for a sphinx. They are hairless and wrinkled and always look like they were just born
PREPPIE	American shorthairs
PRESLEY	For an Elvis fan
PRESSROOM	A very busy animal
PRESTO	A Devon rex (hairless)
PRESTON	Collies (they can't all be Lassie)
PRETTY WOMAN	You like both the song and the movie
PRETZEL	For an animal that turns you inside out
PRIAM	Last king of Troy during the Trojan war

PRIDE	You've decided you like it better than your own children
PRIMA BALLERINA	Exotic shorthairs
PRIMO	The best
PRIMROSE	Another flower . . . remember the song "Primrose Lane" by Pat Boone?
PRINCE	Once every girl's dream . . . to marry a prince and ride off into the sunset
PRINCE CHARMING	Cinderella's knight in shining armor
PRINCE CHARLES	Cinderella's ex-knight in shining armor
PRINCE OF TIDES	The prince that swarm away
PRINCE VALIANT	The prince no one's seemed to find yet
PRINCESS	Once upon a time a beautiful dream . . . today a can of worms
PRINCESS DI	Just ask her!
PRINTER	A pet that makes an impression
PRINTOUT	Mynah birds, parrots
PRISCILLA	I once baby-sat for Priscilla Poodle . . . a mini who was simply charming. Or, it's another choice for Elvis fans
PRISSIE	Priscilla's nickname
PRO	Nickname for a pet on the show circuit
PROFESSOR	You have a very smart pet
PROKOFIEV	Russian composer . . . Sergey. A Borzoi would be wonderful
PROM	You went, loved it, and don't want to forget it
PROMETHEUS	Something about Fire for Mankind and vultures eating his liver as punishment. Heavy stuff for a small pet
PROOF	An alcoholic's pet
PROUST	Either a literary pet or one that dances

PROVENCE   You love the south of France (as well you should)!

PROWLER   A cat or dog with dark circles around its eyes

PROZAC   It used to be depressed, and now it's a pleasure

PRUDENCE   A pet you bought carefully

PRUNELLA   Pugs, bulldogs, boxers

PSYCHO   You'll know if it fits

PUCCI   Designer—still in business after all these years . . . same weird color combinations

PUCCINI   Giacomo. Classical composer. Famous for operas . . . any 'pooch' will do

PUCK   A hockey fan's pet

PUDDING   There seems to be a run of 'Pudding' for Yorkshire terriers

PUDDLES   A dog who has been having problems with housebreaking

PUDGY   If the shoe fits

PUFF   For a Magic Dragon

PUIFORCAT   For a very sweet, dessertish cat

PULITZER   A prizewinning pet

PUMPERNICKEL   For any of your dark brown to black pets

PUMPKIN   An orange-and-black tabby, or an American wirehair

PUNCH   Pair with Judy

PUNKY   *Punky Brewster* . . . TV show . . . all grown up now

PUREE   A cook's pet

PURPLE PASSION   A pet that drives one to such lengths that the purple vein in your neck sticks out!

PURRFECT   For the perfect cat

PURRFECTLY SWEET Too syrupy

PURRY FURRY
BETSEY ROSS   A winner at the Madison Square Garden
                       Cat Show

PUSHKIN   Pugs, bulldogs, boxers
PUSS-IN-BOOTS   A cat with mittens
PUSSYWILLOW   Perfect for spotted tabbies
PUTTER   A golfer's pet
PUZO   Your pet will have a godfather
PYEWACKET   The cat from *Bell, Book & Candle*
PYGMALION   For a pet that you got from the pound
                       that turned out to be a pedigree

QANTAS	Koalas
QUACK	A doctor's pet
QUAGOE	You love the Hamptons
QUAID	A Dennis or Randy fan
QUAINT	A nice, old-fashioned pet
QUAKER	A gentle pet
QUANTUM LEAPER	For a time traveler
QUARANTINE	Your pet is always sick
QUARK	A very, very tiny pet
QUARTERBACK	It's always barking orders
QUARTZ	Takes a licking and keeps on ticking
QUASAR	You just like the way it sounds
QUASI	Almost
QUASIMODO	Turtles, shar-peis, pugs, bulldogs, reptiles
QUAYLE	You're a potatoe lover
QUE SERA SERA	You're not sure it's a pedigree . . . but you're relaxed about it

QUEASY	You're not sure it's a pedigree . . . and you're sick about it
QUEEN	A pet with a superiority complex
QUEEN ANNE	Your pet loves to sit on the furniture
QUEEN ELIZABETH	A pet with family problems
QUEEN ISABELLA	A pet that finances explorers
QUEEN LATIFAH	A pet that likes to rap
QUEENIE	Michael Korda's book. Great pet name
QUENCHER	A pet into Gatorade
QUENTIN	A pet that understands *Pulp Fiction*
QUESADILLA	You love Mexican food
QUEST	American foxhounds, bloodhounds, coonhounds, etc.
QUETZAL	For a sweet, affectionate female
QUEUE	An English duck with its babies
QUIBBLER	A pet you can never satisfy
QUICHE	Your male pet won't eat it
QUICK	It's very smart
QUICKEN	A pet good in accounting
QUICKIE	Rabbits
QUICKSAND	A pet that might eventually turn on you
QUIET	You barely know it's there
QUIGLY	Rhymes with wiggly . . . snakes
QUILL	Birds
QUINCE	A pet into exotic fruit
QUINCY	For an aspiring coroner
QUININE	A soothing pet
QUINN	A mighty pet
QUIPSTER	It's a comedian and it never stops
QUIRK	It has a tick
QUIXOTE	It's a dreamer

QUIZ	For the pet that keeps you guessing
QUIZZIE	For a little pet that keeps you guessing
QUOTA	You swear it's your last pet
QUOTH	Don't quoth me

R2D2	You have an obedient pet
RACER	A sailer's pet
RACEWAY	Greyhounds
RADAR	For a *M*A*S*H* lover or an air traffic controller
RADCLIFFE	Pair with Harvard
RADIO	You grew up in the '40s
RAGA	You have an Indian pet
RAGGEDY ANDY	Male ragdolls
RAGGEDY ANN	Female ragdolls
RAGING BULL	Boxers, bulls
RAGS	Sloppy pets
RAGTIME	Your pet has a blanky
RAGU	Saucy pets
RAGWEED	For pets with runny eyes
RAIL	Your pet is as skinny as a . . .
RAILWAY	A conductor's pet
RAIN	Any of the water spaniels
RAINBOW	Mixed breeds
RAINER	Perhaps, a Great Spitz. (Get it?)

RAINWATER	Your pet won't drink from the toilet
RAINY	Your dog drools
RAISIN BREAD	A brown-and-white pet?
RAJA	A posh Indian of great standing
RAKE	Definitely a male, non-neutered, traveling man
RALEIGH	A smoker's pet
RALPH	A wonderful pet name . . . Ralph Kramden . . . *The Honeymooners*
RAMBO	Guard dogs
RAMON	What a fabulous name—how about for a pet that looks like it has a mustache?
RAMSEY	A strong name for a strong pet
RANDALL	A more selective 'Randy'
RANDY	A pet who's always ready for anything . . . another un-neutered male
RANGE ROVER	A pet that can travel anywhere
RANGER	For a pet that roams your land or plays hockey
RAOUL	A cannibal's pet
RAPUNZEL	A puli would be perfection
RAQUEL	It would have to be a sexy animal, whatever it was
RASHID	A pet that you're allergic to
RASKOLNIKOV	For the pet with a guilty conscience
RASPBERRY	Reddish pets would be adorable
RASTA	A puli you have no intention of combing
RATHBONE	A pet that loves basil
RATTATOUILLE	Perfect for a mutt
RAVEL	Your pet wears a bolero
RAVIOLI	Stuffed pasta. A bichon frise!
RAY	One cool dude . . . sunglasses, possibly a hat . . . definitely connected
RAY CHARLES	For a singing pet that wants to do Pepsi commercials

RAYON	Someone in the rag trade could really do something with this name
RAZOOK	For a pet that shrieks
RAZZ	Your pet is fresh
RAZZMATAZZ	A flashy pet that looks good in a sequin collar
REAGAN	For the pet that turns out differently than you expected
REAL ESTATE	It came as part of the deal
REBECCA	You'll be living on Sunnybrook Farm
REBEL	You were a hood in the '60s
RECALL	A pet for a person who would like to remember the '60s
RECCA	A nice way of naming an animal that wrecks your house
RECUPERATE	For someone partial to the ocean
RECYCLE	A pet from the pound
RED	Red setters
RED CROSS	A red setter who thinks it's a Saint Bernard
RED E	For setters that are always eager
RED EYE	Bicoastal red setters
RED FIELD	Formal red setters
RED RIDING HOOD	A red setter that's always visiting its grandmother
RED SEA	A setter who thinks it's Moses
REDCLOUD	A setter who lives on a reservation
REDFORD	A setter who likes acting as your director
REDFURR	A well-groomed red setter
REDNECK	A red setter who only lives with its own kind
REDWOOD	A setter who thinks it's exceptionally tall
REESE'S PIECE	Spotted tabbies, Egyptian maus
REFRIGERATOR	For the pet that loves its food

REFRY	A good name for a fish
REGGIE	You love baseball
REGIS	Pair with Kathie Lee
REILLY	For someone who wants 'the life of . . . '
REISS	Iceland dogs, cockatoos
RELAY	Race dogs
RELISH	A pet you got to go with your dachshund
REMBRANDT	For an artistic Dutch sheepdog
REMINGTON	A pet of 'Steele'
REMOTE CONTROL	For a pet who obeys when you call it
REMUS	Pair with Romulus
REMY	Nice easy name
REMY MARTIN	Let's face it, you like to drink now and then
RENNIE	Very cute name
RENO	Your ex gave it to you
RENOIR	A painter's pet
REPETE	Pair with Pete
REPLAY	See Recall
REPORTER	A newsperson's pet
REQUIEM	For a heavyweight
RESCUE	Saint Bernard or any pet you get from the pound
RESCUER	Same . . . but, it finds YOU
RESEARCH	You can never find it easily
RETAIL	You paid through the nose
RETREAD	An older dog from the pound
REUBEN	It makes you think of a sandwich
REUTERS	A Russian wolfhound into the news
REVEREND	A black cat with a white collar
REWIND	Good name for anyone in the audio or video business
REX	Now here's an original name

RHAPSODY	For any of your 'Blue' breeds
RHETT	A dashing pet who doesn't give a damn
RHETT BUTLER	A dashing pet who doesn't give a damn and prefers a proper introduction
RHINESTONE COWBOY	Dalmatians. We'll pretend that all those spots are rhinestones
RHUBARB	For a sourpuss
RHYMER	A poet's pet
RHYTHM	A musician's pet
RIBBON	Snakes
RIBBONS	A winner's pet
RICARDO	Pair with McGillicudy
RICHARD	Strange name for a pet. But, anything's possible
RICK	Richard's nickname. For a *Casablanca* fan . . . pair with Ilsa
RICKLES	For an acerbic pet
RICKRACK	A seamstress's pet
RICKSHAW	One of the Chinese dogs. A Shih Tzu or Lhasa
RICKY	Lucy's sweetheart
RIDDLER	Your pet enjoys giving you trouble
RIDDLES	An obnoxious joke person's pet
RIGHTY	A pet that's never wrongy
RILEY	For a William Bendix fan
RIN TIN TIN	This is, actually, a very weird name
RINGLING BROTHERS	If you can get all your pets to do the same trick simultaneously
RIO	For a Grande pet
RIP	Guard dogs
RIP VAN WINKLE	A guard dog that sleeps on the job
RIPLEY	For someone with 10 cats and gets another . . . believe it or not

RIPTIDE	You have a fast turtle
RISKY	A Yugoslavian tricolor hound. Anything from Yugoslavia is a bit risky right now
RISQUÉ	A hairless dog (Cane Nudo). That's the name. And it's found in Mexico
RITALIN	It has helped someone in your family, and you want to honor it
RITZ	Possibility for a parrot. Ritz, as in cracker, as in 'Polly'
RIVA	For someone with an accent
RIVER	Portuguese, American, and Irish water spaniels
RIXON	Son of Rick
RIZZO	Good for hamsters or rats
ROAD RUNNER	A jogger's bird
ROAMER	See Rake
ROB ROY	A pet that fights for what it believes in
ROBERT REDFURR	Someone really named their cat this
ROBERTA	For a pet that gives no Flack
ROBIN	My friend and superb anestheseologist at Columbia Presbyterian
ROBIN HOOD	A pet that takes your belongings and brings them to your less fortunate neighbors
ROBINSON CRUSOE	Your pet can fend for itself
ROCCO	Another connected guy. Older than Ray
ROCHESTER	Jack Benny's sidekick
ROCK	For a strong, immovable animal
ROCK 'N' ROLL	You'll always love it
ROCKET J. SQUIRREL	Pair with Bullwinkle
ROCKETTE	Pets with particularly great legs
ROCKWELL	A pet for someone named Norman or an engineer

ROCKY	Sylvester Stallone
ROCKY II	Sylvester Stallone
ROCKY III	Sylvester Stallone
ROCKY IV	Sylvester Stallone
ROCKY MOUNTAIN HIGH	Sylve . . . (oops) John Denver
ROCKY ROAD	A Russian wolfhound and an American shorthaired pointer mix
RODIN	An artist's pet
RODNEY	Cocker Spaniels, dachshunds
ROGER	Ann Margret's favorite pet
ROGER RABBIT	Rabbits
ROGET	The pet you depend on when writing
ROGUE	This reminds me of the movie with David Niven. Chicly naughty
ROLAND	A great, big briard
ROLEX	When you can't buy one
ROLLER	A pet who likes the high life
ROLLER SKATE	A pet that likes the cold life
ROLLERBLADE	A pet that likes the fast life
ROLLO	For a pet that May
ROLLO MAY	For the pet that will help you be your best self
ROLY-POLY	Your pet will start out fat and stay that way
ROMAINE	A pet that likes green vegetables
ROMAN	For an Italian pointer
ROMEO	Pair with Juliet. Shakespeare would be happy, but the Capulets will be upset with you
ROMI	Your pet hates to stay home
ROMULUS	Pair with Remus
RONALD	Nancy won't like you
RONDA	My sister-in-law in Boston. HI Ronda!! Mother of Mandy, Brooke, and Rebecca
RONNIE	Ronald's nickname

RONNO	For a disobedient Ron
ROOFER	For a dog that goes "Roof Roof." (Sorry)
ROOSEVELT	I like this name. It has character
ROPER	A cowboy's pet
RORSCHACH	A pet whose markings always remind you of something
ROSA	Your Spanish pet looks good with one between its teeth
ROSANNA	For a pet with a sweet, kind disposition
ROSANNADANNA	You watch *Saturday Night Live* reruns
ROSANNE	Your pet tells it like it is
ROSCOE	This reminds me of someone at the track. So, I would say, a better's pet
ROSE	Your American pet looks good with one between its teeth
ROSEDALE	A pet from the suburbs
ROSENKRANTZ	Pair with Guildenstern
ROSIE	In my opinion, one of the nicer female names
ROSIE O'GRADY	Another good name for a Great Dane, or any other large animals
ROSIE THE RIVETER	Female bulldogs
ROSKO	A wirehaired fox terrier, or any frisky pet
ROTINI	More pasta
ROULETTE	Any caged animal that has a wheel
ROUSSEAU	A jungle animal
ROVER	Well, if you really must!
ROWDY	Bosnian hounds
ROWENA	Oriental shorthair whites
ROWF	You let the dog name itself
ROWSER	You will depend on this pet to wake you up
ROXANNE	Pair with Cyrano

ROXETTE	An ex-Rockette
ROXI	For an old movie aficionado
ROY	My cousin Robin in Connecticut's husband
ROY BOY	What she calls him
ROY ROGERS	Dale Evans's and Trigger's best friend
ROYCE	Rolls's last name
ROZA	A South American pet looks good with one between its teeth
ROZEN	My dermatologist
RUBLE	A worthless pet
RUBY	For pets born in July
RUBY FRUIT	For a July pet with exotic tastes
RUDEBOY	For a fresh and sassy pet
RUDOLPH	If you have a reindeer or a red nose— perfection
RUDY	Hamsters, mice, lizards, snakes
RUFF	Dennis the Menace's dog
RUFFER	A roofer's pet
RUFFHAUSER	Rottweilers, German shepherds, vizslas, any pet that plays too hard
RUFFIAN	A pet with a dirty-looking face
RUFUS	Such a perfect animal name
RUGBY	Your pet looks good in shorts
RUGGELAH	Your pet gains weight over the holidays
RUGGLES	A pet who waddles . . . especially appropriate for short-legged varieties
RUM	Pair with Coke
RUMBA	Great name for a dachshund. Can't you just picture those tiny legs swinging around?
RUMMY	For a pet that loves gin
RUMOR	A mynah bird who loves gossip
RUMPELSTILTSKIN	Another good name for the shar-pei
RUNNER	Greyhounds
RUNWAY	A pilot's pet

RUNYON	Racing animals
RUPERT	You always dreamed of being a media mogul
RUSH	A mynah bird with two right wings
RUSHMORE	Pets with granite faces
RUSS	A short athletic type
RUSSELL	The second most favorite name of the Jack Russell terrier. The first, as you can guess, is Steve. Just kidding
RUSTY	Always makes me think of *The Danny Thomas Show*
RUTHIE	My cousin who just moved to Buenos Aires
RYAN	The pet for which you have Hope
RYDER	This always makes me think of Ryder Fitzgerald and his sister Desmi, who went to school with me
RYE	Pair with Hamon
RYLEE	An Irish terrier with a southern accent

SA CAS TIC	Bulldogs, pugs, shar-peis
SABATINI	You're into tennis
SABE	I used to baby-sit for his children and be terrified to walk home alone. They lived right next door
SABERT	What his children called him
SABIN	An inoculator's pet
SABRINA	You have a remake
SABU	For big, clumsy-looking pets like Saint Bernards, Clumber spaniels, Newfoundlands
SADAT	For an Egyptian sphinx
SADIE	Married lady
SADIE HAWKINS	Feline seeking male companion
SAFARI	You have a wild cat
SAFIRE	An opinionated pet
SAGAN	An extraterrestrial pet
SAGE	A very wise pet
SAGGY	Perfect for basset hounds
SAHARA	Camels, lizards, snakes

SAHL	Comic dog from the Lenny Bruce era
SAILOR	For a black-and-white animal . . . mostly white
SAINT	Only you know if it applies
SAINT LAURENT	Your pet walks like it's on a runway
SAINT-TROPEZ	A topless pet
SAL	Your pet eats pizza
SALAZAR	A long-distance runner
SALES	A salesman's pet
SALINGER	French bulldogs or hermits
SALISBURY	For a pet into steak
SALK	Your pet understands the value of inoculations
SALLY	And Buddy. *The Dick Van Dyke Show*
SALOME	Your pet needs seven veils
SALVADOR	For a Dalí
SAM	A no-nonsense pet
SAM SPADE	A no-nonsense neutered pet that does detective work on the side
SAM WAH	A no-nonsense Chinese crested pet
SAMANTHA	A no-nonsense female Sam's formal name
SAMBA	Your 'Sam' can dance
SAMMY	What you call the no-nonsense Sam when you're happy with him
SAMPRAS	Tennis again
SAMSON	For any of the very big (or very small), very long-(or very short-) hair breeds . . . preferably shaggy
SAN PELLEGRINO	Your pet only drinks bottled water
SAND	A pet that sticks in your craw
SANDBURG	A poet's pet
SANDER	A floor finisher's pet
SANDERS	A colonel's pet

SANDOR	For someone with very clear pronunciation
SANDY	My brother in Boston. He has three daughters and a dog named Snickers
SANIBEL	It's an island pet
SANTA	For a jolly, fat pet
SANTA CLAW	For a jolly, fat pet with claws
SANTA FE	An artist's pet partial to turquoise
SANTANA	A guitarist's pet
SAPPHIRE	From the TV show *Amos and Andy*
SAPPHO	A-museing pet
SARABETH	A pet with braids
SARAH	Blue-cream point Himalayans . . . no braids
SARATOGA	Race horses
SARATOGA TRUNK	Elephants who race
SARAZEN	Golfing pets
SARGENT	Guard dogs
SARNO	Pets with good skin
SARNOFF	Pets that like to watch TV
SAROYAN	Borzois, Russian blues, Russian wolfhounds, etc.
SARTO	For an artsy pet
SARTRE	An existential pet
SASHA	Russian birds into teasing helpless wolves
SASHIMI	One of my ex-husband's cats . . . paired with Sushi
SASSAFRAS	For a pet with a keen sense of smell
SASSOON	For a pet that likes to go to the groomer often
SASSY	Pets that talk back
SATCHEL	A pet that's going to be carried around a lot
SATCHMO	A Newfoundland with a raspy voice

SATIE	For the pet who loves French composers
SATIRE	A mangy pet, but, you insist on sequined collar and pink bows for its hair
SAUCERS	Pets with big eyes
SAUL	A pet that bellows
SAUVIGNON	A wine lover's pet
SAVALAS	You're into bald eagles and lollipops
SAVANNAH	A pet from Georgia
SAUVIGNON BLANC	White pets
SAWYER	Tomcats
SAY SO	Your pet likes the last word
SAY WHAT	Your pet acts like it's hard of hearing
SCAASI	A designer's pet
SCANDAL	What you get when you cross a pedigree with a mixed breed
SCARECROW	And Mrs. King
SCARLATTI	For a pet with papers
SCARLETT	Willful pets
SCARLETT O'HARA	Willful pets with good taste in men
SCAVULLO	Your pet likes to have its picture taken
SCHEHERAZADE	Your pet really knows how to tell a story
SCHELL	A fancy fish
SCHIAPARELLI	A designer's pet
SCHIPA	A Dutch border collie . . . with its own flock
SCHIPPERS	You work for a moving company
SCHLEMMER	Hammacher's partner
SCHLESINGER	For a very formal, politically minded person
SCHMIDT	Dobermans, German shepherds, German pointers
SCHMOODER	For one of the very hyper terriers
SCHNAPPSIE	Schnauzers who drink
SCHNEIDER	A superintendent's pet

SCHOONER	A sailor's pet
SCHOPENHAUER	For one of the giant breeds, preferably German, preferably philosophical
SCHUBERT	Alley cats
SCHULTZ	Pair with Hogan or Klink
SCHULZ	For a *Peanuts* fan
SCHUMANN	A musician's pet
SCHUSTER	Pair with Simon
SCHWARZENEGGER	Another one for giant breeds, preferably Austrian, preferably guard dogs
SCHWEITZER	African tsetse flies
SCONE	You enjoyed high tea in England
SCOOBY DOO	A cartoon character in the form of a dog
SCOOP	A journalist's pet
SCOOT	Scooter's nickname
SCOOTER	You like pie
SCORSESE	A director's pet
SCOTCH	A drinker's pet
SCOTT	Scottish terriers
SCOTTIE	A Scottish terrier would be the obvious choice, for a person with sinus problems, less obvious
SCOTTO	A good-ol'-boy Scottish terrier
SCOUNDREL	For that naughty Scottish terrier
SCOUT	American bloodhounds, any of the hunters
SCRABBLE	You think it's smarter than you are
SCRAMBLER	Your pet slides on the hardwood floor
SCRUNCH	Tawny boxers, shar-peis, Pekingese, or pugs
SE WAT	Parrots, mynahs, macaws
SEA BREEZE	Great drink, mellow atmosphere, good memories
SEAGRAM	More serious than Sea Breeze
SÉANCE	Black cats

SEBASTIAN	My sister-in-law, Marilyn, had two Old English sheepdogs . . . both were named Sebastian
SEDAKA	You've just been through a divorce (Breaking Up is Hard to Do)
SEDONA	A psychic's pet
SEDRICK	One of the great names
SEE TING	For a party planner
SEEGER	A folksinger's pet
SEGA	A New Age game pet
SEGAL	You love the way it walks
SEGOVIA	You love the way it plays
SELES	You also love the way it plays
SELIM	See Vera . . . this is her father
SELLECK	For a very good looking pet that doesn't take itself too seriously
SELMA	A civil rights worker's pet
SELTZER	For a bubbly pet
SELWYN	The name's been in the family for years, and you can't get out of it now
SEÑATE	For a very stately, calm pet
SENATOR	For a not so calm pet that often needs to be leashed
SEÑOR	Spanish mastiffs
SERGEI	Russian wolfhounds
SERLING	For a pet you're beginning to think came from the Twilight Zone
SETTLER	You end up with the runt of the litter
SEUSS	A doctor's pet
SEVAREID	You're into the news
SEVENTH HEAVEN	When you've avoided Settler and gotten your pick
SEVERINSEN	A trumpet playing Doc-shund
SEYMORE	Another for the Seeing Eye dogs
SEYMOUR	A fat pet

SGT. PEPPER	For a lonely heart
SHADE	An evening pet
SHADOW	Follows you wherever you go
SHAH	An exiled pet
SHAKESPEARE	A poetic pet
SHANDLING	You've got HBO
SHANE	Horses
SHANGRI-LA	A pet that's easy to be with
SHANKAR	A Ravi fan
SHANNON	Irish pets
SHAQ	Shaquille O'Neil
SHAQUILLE	Very cool name
SHARIF	An Omar fan
SHATNER	A *Star Trek* fan
SHATZI	Wirehaired fox terriers
SHATZY	Small Swiss hounds
SHAW	Pharaoh hounds . . . docile, loyal, affectionate, and playful
SHAWN	Irish pets
SHEENA	You have the queen of the jungle
SHEEZA BABE	You think it's gorgeous
SHEFFIELD	The father on *The Nanny*
SHEIK	For a very suave pet, preferably with Arabic heritage
SHELBY	An aspiring preppy's pet
SHELDON	A pet that gives you reason to have Memories of Midnight
SHELLY	Cute for fish
SHEP	A name for a German shepherd given by an owner always in a hurry
SHEPHERD	Sheepdogs that look good with a staff
SHERATON	You're partial to hotel names
SHERBERT	Multicolored pets
SHERIDAN	An Ann fan

SHERIFF	Another good name for guard dogs, small cats
SHERMAN	It's built like a tank
SHERWOOD	For a Murphy Brown wanna-be
SHEVARDNADZE	For any of the Russian breeds
SHIH LIANG	For any of the Chinese breeds
SHINER	Your pet has one black eye
SHIRAZ	A city in Iran
SHIRLEY	Shirley basset hound
SHISHKEBAB	For any of the breeds with particularly short legs . . . dachshunds, corgis, etc.
SHOCKING BLUE	You thought it was going to be a red point Birman
SHOCKING PINK	You thought it was going to be a blue point Birman
SHOGUN	Any of the Japanese breeds
SHOOKER	A pet you always have to wake up
SHOOTING PAIN	Your pet bites indiscriminately
SHORTIE	Any short pet or, to be contrary, any very tall pet
SHOW-OFF	Your pet always takes first prize, then brags about it
SHOWBOAT	Your pet always takes first prize, then YOU brag about it
SHRIMP	The mini breeds, silky terriers, Chihuahuas, cairn terriers
SHRIVER	Pam, Sargent, and Eunice
SHUBI	You're partial to '50s songs
SICILY	Italian greyhounds, very proud of their heritage
SID	Nondenominational and adorable
SIDNEY	Nondenominational, and still adorable
SIEGFRIED	Pair with Roy
SIEPI	Italian hounds . . . vivacious but undemonstrative in affection

SIGGI	For a small spitz . . . affectionate with family, suspicious of strangers
SIGMUND	A therapist's pet
SIGNORET	A pet for a Simone
SILICONE	Either a Valley pet, or one with implants
SILKY	Any of the silky terriers
SILVER SPIRIT	You had a pet named Silver and this one is named in its honor
SIMBA	A pet from the jungle
SIMMONS	For a bubbly, bouncy pet that's into dieting
SIMON	A pet that makes you do as it says
SIMONE	My ex-husband's new wife's daughter . . . lovely, lives in California
SIMPSON	For a pet that can keep a straight face under any circumstances
SINATRA	Your pet has blue eyes
SINBAD	A sailor's pet
SINCLAIR	Good name . . . for strong, dependable pets, Pyrenees mastiffs, Newfoundlands, American foxhounds
SINGER	Birds . . . or else, you're a tailor
SINSO	Is my cat Homer's brother
SIR ARTHUR	Your pet will be eating at a round table
SIR FON	Fish
SIR LOIN	Cows and pigs
SIR STUD	For a prolific pet with class
SIREN	Pets that howl
SISLEY	For someone in the Tie business
SITTING BULL	Sitting Bulls
SKEET	A shooter's pet
SKEET SHOOT	Ducks
SKEETER	Because your heart MUST go on beating, that's why
SKELETON	Devon rex or greyhounds
SKELTON	Red pets

SKIPPER	You still watch *Gilligan's Island*
SKIPPY	You love peanut butter
SKY	A pilot's pet
SKY KING	You have over 1 million frequent flier miles . . . or, you remember the old TV series
SLATER	A mason's pet
SLEEPING BEAUTY	Your pet naps a lot, but watch those apples
SLESS	Schlesinger's nickname
SLIM	Greyhounds
SLIM PICKINS	What's left of the Greyhound's litter
SLOAN'S	A supermarket I worked in the summer before I went to college
SLY	Sneaky pets
SMART E	Parrots, mynahs
SMIRNOFF	Less expensive than Stoli
SMITH	Your pet prefers to be incognito
SMITHIE	The incognito pet who wants a nickname
SMITS	Police dogs
SMITTIE	Another friend from high school. She was a cheerleader too
SMOCKING	Tabbys
SMOKEY	Perfect for a Newfoundland, or someone named Robinson
SMYTH	A fancy Smith
SMYTHE	A fancy English Smith
SNAPPLE	Your pet drinks a lot
SNEAKERS	Your pet creeps up on you all the time
SNOOPY	Is he a beagle?
SNOW WHITE	The last and largest in a litter of eight tiny white animals
SNOWFLAKE	An all-white kitten who's one of a kind
SNOWMAN	Siberian huskies

SNOWSHOE	Eskimo dogs
SNOWBALL	For an all-white kitten . . . and, don't forget—it was the prizewinning name I told you about in the intro
SNOWDEN	Lord, I don't know
SNYDER	Giant schnauzers
SO BIG	Yorkies
SOCKS	Any pet with markings around its paws
SOCRATES	Any pet that thinks a lot
SODA	Companion to Scotch
SOHO	For a trendy pet from New York City
SOJOURNER	Tomcats
SOLACE	The pet you buy to replace someone
SOLDIER	Boxers, bulldogs
SOLO	Your pet likes to be alone
SOLO MAN	For a one-pet family
SOLOMON	For a serious pet
SOLZHENITSYN	Another name for any of the Russian breeds
SONA	A cocker spaniel whose nickname is Precious
SONAR	Pet bats
SONDHEIM	It will want to be on Broadway
SONTAG	A black pet with a white streak
SOON PENG	Akitas, Tibetan mastiffs, shar-peis, etc.
SOOPURR	You have a great cat
SOPHIE	You had a choice
SOPHOCLES	A pet into drama or Greek tragedies
SOUFFLÉ	For someone into desserts
SOUPY	For someone into soups
SOURDOUGH	For someone into breads
SOUSA	For someone into bands
SPACEY	For someone into drugs
SPALDING	For someone into tennis
SPARKIE	For someone into matches

SPARKLE	For someone into fireworks
SPARKS	For someone into fires
SPARKY	For someone into starting fires
SPECTATOR	For someone into voyeurism
SPECTRUM	For someone into colors
SPECULATOR	For someone into the stock market
SPENDER	For someone into shopping
SPENSER	For someone into detectives
SPIDERMAN	For someone into climbing walls
SPIEGEL	For someone into catalog shopping
SPIKE	For a Dandie Dinmont terrier (has just one tuft of hair on its head)
SPIKE LEE	For a Dandie Dinmont that directs movies
SPILLANE	A detective's pet . . . for a macho hunting dog that wears a hat indoors
SPINOZA	A philosopher's pet
SPIRIT	For a make-believe pet
SPIVAK	For any of the Russian breeds
SPLASH	Fish . . . or, how you know the cat's in the fish tank again
SPOCK	A Vulcan breed with big, pointy ears
SPODE	A delicate, almost breakable pet
SPOILER	For a bratty bulldog
SPOOK	Mrs. Muir's captain
SPOOKIE	That Mrs. Muir HAD a captain
SPORT	A jock's pet
SPOT	Belongs to Dick and Jane
SPRING	For any pet that arrived the early part of the year
SPRINGSTEEN	The Boss pet
SPRITE	Your pet likes clear sodas
SPUTNIK	An astronaut's pet
SPY	A mysterious pet
SPYMASTER	The most mysterious pet

SQUASH	A flat pet
SQUAW	An Indian pet
SQUEAK	A tiny pet
SQUEAKIE	A teeny pet
SQUIRT	A small pet
ST. JAMES	A religious pet
STACKER	A strong pet
STADIUM	A mascot
STAKEOUT	A very patient watchdog
STALACTITE	A pet with floppy ears
STALAGMITE	A pet with pointy ears
STALLONE	A rocky pet
STANLEY	A Ranger's pet
STANWYCK	A dramatic pet
STAR	A famous pet
STARBUCK	A famous pet into coffee
STARDUST	A famous dead pet
STARFIRE	A rising famous pet
STARFROST	An outdoor famous pet
STARR	An extra famous pet
STEELE	You loved *Remington Steele*
STEINBECK	For a red pony or a pet partial to grapes
STELLA	A *Streetcar* fan
STERLING	Your pet will eat from a silver bowl
STETHOSCOPE	Pet snakes with sensitive hearing
STETSON	The pet who looks good in cowboy hats
STEVENS	For a *Bewitched* fan
STEVENSON	A Democrat's pet . . . pair with Eisenhower
STEWARD	For someone who likes to take cruises
STEWART	For someone who likes Martha
STING	For someone who likes bees
STOCKARD	Guard dogs
STOCKWELL	A dean's pet
STOKES	A pet into fires

STOLI	See Smirnoff
STONE	This is for one tough pet
STONY	One very stubborn pet
STORMIN' NORMAN	You rely on it to protect you
STÖSSEL	Your pet seeks the truth
STRADIVARIUS	A pet that is in tune with you
STRADIVARI	A pair of pets in tune with you
STRAUSS	Your pet can waltz
STRAVINSKY	A musician's pet
STRAWBERRY	An athlete's pet, a cook's pet, or your pet's in rehab
STREEP	A cat that's such a good actress that you sometimes think it's a dog
STREISAND	A ballad-belting Afghan that pays close attention to details
STRETCH	A limo-riding dachshund
STRITCH	For a baby limo-riding dachshund
STUART	Scottish clan dogs . . . pretensions to the throne
STUDS	For a flashy pet . . . sort of a rhinestone cowboy
STURGES	Another good Scottish name for someone into "they don't make 'em like that anymore" movies
STUTZ	A Bearcat
STUYVESANT	You bought it for $24.00
SUDS	A clean pet
SUE	For a boy named
SUE PERB	Sue's full name
SUEDE	Any of the blue breeds
SUEY PING	An Eastern pet
SUGAR	A Southern pet
SUGAR RAY	A boxer
SUGARLOAF	A skier's pet
SUKI	An Asian pet

SULLIVAN	An Irish pet
SULLY	An Italian pet
SULTAN	An Arab pet
SULTAN OF SWAT	Babe Ruth's nickname
SULTANA	A yellow wrinkled pet
SUMMER	A hot pet
SUMMER BREEZE	A hot pet with a cool temperament
SUMMER STOCK	A revival pet
SUMO	A Japanese fighting pet
SUN DANCE	A pet from a rainy climate
SUN RA	A jazz musician's pet
SUN YAT-SEN	Pets into Chinese history
SUNBONNET	Pets with flat tops and bushy eyebrows
SUNFLOWER	Pets with big faces and a crown of hair
SUNG	Pets with big lungs
SUNNY	A friend who, since I've known her, has had a Honey, Bristol, Brie, Wheatly, and Josie
SUNRISE	A pet shaded from red to orange to yellow
SUNRISE, SUNSET	For a pair from the shelter
SUNSET	A pet shaded from yellow to orange to red
SUNSHINE	A pet without PMS
SUPERMAN	A pet that doesn't mind hanging out with a non-sunshine animal
SURE BET	Greyhounds
SURPRISE	For the unexpected addition
SUSHI	Pair with Sashimi
SUSSKIND	For someone into Davids
SUTHERLAND	For someone into Donalds
SUZANNAH	For someone into banjos
SUZETTE	For someone into crêpes

SUZUKI	For someone into motorcycles
SVENGALI	An older pet you're still breeding
SVETLANA	For someone into Russians
SWAYZE	For someone into dancing
SWEET GEORGIA BROWN	For someone into golden oldies
SWEET GINGER BROWN	You loved *Flamingo Kid*
SWEET PEA	Popeye's baby
SWEET POTATO	For red pets . . . red Abyssinians, Oriental reds, Irish setters
SWEET WILLIAM	For any sweet-looking, mellow pet
SWEETIE PIE	For a pet with just a little of the rascal in it
SWEETHEART	You're a sentimentalist
SWIFT	A pet for an Oliver
SWIFTIE	Another good Greyhound name
SWIFTY	A pet just this side of the law
SWISS BLISS	A chocolate lover's pet
SWISS MISS	A hot chocolate lover's pet
SWIT	Another name for a *M*A*S*H* fan
SWOOZIE	For a pet who faints easily
SYBIL	Your pet has multiple personalities
SYLVESTER	Cats
SYLVIA	Another of my favorite female names

3-D	For a pet whose eyes are two different colors
T.C.	The Cat
T.J.	Tough, athletic type
T.R.	The Runt
TAB	A hunter's pet
TABBY	Striped cats
TABITHA	Striped cats with stuck-up tails and a lisp
TABLESPOON	Big animals who share your food at mealtimes
TACO	For anyone who loves Mexican food
TAFFETA	An animal that rustles as it goes by
TAFFY	What girls aged five to eight name their cocker spaniels
TAFT	U.S. president 1909–1913. Chief justice 1921–1930
TAGS	A pet that won't leave your side. Either that or it bears a strong resemblance to your luggage
TAI CHI	Chow Chows, Pekingese, Siamese, etc.

TAI PAN	A Chinese Imperial Ch'in . . . the leader . . .
TAIGA	For a tiger with a New York accent
TAILOR	Best used in collections . . . companions are Tinker, Soldier, and Spy
TAJ	For a Ma Hal
TAKAHO	Japanese spitz, Japanese bobtails
TAKEOUT	A city pet
TALBOT	Old English sheepdogs, Irish wolfhounds
TALLCHIEF	The female American ballet dancer . . . though she's American, an Afghan would be perfect
TALLEYRAND	The French statesman (1754–1838)
TALLULAH	For your most dramatic pet
TALMUD	For a Yiddish owl
TAM O' SHANTER	Scotties
TAMALE	For a hot Chihuahua
TAMARA	One of my grandmothers . . . (not the one I watched TV with—that was Gladys)
TAMBOURINE	Those with collars holding many I.D. tags
TAMIL	Indian and Sri Lankan race and language
TAMMY	Cute and bouncy . . . like a bichon frise
TAN POY	Chinese crested dogs
TANDY	A pet that mates for life
TANGLEWOOD	Pulis
TANGO	You two should be very close
TANK	Guard dogs. A tough guy's companion
TANKARD	Your drinking companion
TANKER	A nice, fat pet
TANKER RAY	A nice, fat pet named Ray, that drinks gin

TANTE	German shepherds or German pointers . . . means 'aunt' in German
TANTRA	A cat name
TANTRUM	For the cat who acts out
TANYA	A competitive pet, though not a recommended ASA show animal
TAO	A pet with many secrets
TAOS	Reptiles
TAPESTRY	For animals with coats that tell a story
TAPIOCA	Off-white with little fur balls
TAPPER	Any cat with socks
TAP SHOE	A pet whose nails are left unclipped
TARA	Home for Scarlett
TARGET	Dalmatians and leopards
TARIFF	Expensive and imported
TARKINGTON	American writer . . . perfect for a Newfoundland . . . big dog, big name
TAROT	A symbolic pet
TARRAGON	An animal partial to meat and poultry
TARZAN	It keeps going out looking for Jane
TASHI	Lhasa Apsos
TASTER	Any pet that shares your food
TATE	For a lovable but slightly dingy pet (I loved *Soap* and Jessica Tate)
TATER TOT	One of Tate's kids
TATI	A tall French poodle who is funny (French director and actor Jacques Tati)
TATIANA	For a pet that smells good
TATTOO	A pet with distinctive markings . . . at least one of which looks like a heart with the word 'MOM' in it
TAURUS	For a very stubborn pet, or one born in May
TAX SHELTER	A very expensive animal you can write off
TAXI	Horses, mules, elephants, or camels

TAYLOR	For an Elizabeth, Robert, Renee, Zachary, or Miss Taylor (your third-grade teacher)
TAZZA	For a miniature breed . . . something that can fit in a cup
TCHAIKOVSKY	Borzois, Russian blues, and Swans
TEA BISCUIT	Lapdogs
TEACHER'S PET	When you've chosen the runt of the litter
TEAPOT	An animal with a stiff tail
TEASDALE	American poet . . . a pet that plays hide and seek
TEASPOON	Little animals that share your food at mealtimes
TECUMSEH	Parrots, macaws, etc.
TED	For a no-nonsense animal
TEDDY	Softer and cuter than Ted
TEDDY BEAR	Softer and cuter than Teddy
TEENY-WEENY	One of those double names whose second half you'll never get around to using
TEKA MAKI	For a fish that won't be cooked
TELEGRAM	For a homing pigeon
TELEPATHY	For a pet that anticipates your every command
TELEX	The homing pigeon's younger brother
TELLER	Caged animals
TELLY	Shaved head, likes lollipops
TEMPEST	Any pet that fits in a teapot
TEMPLETON	*Simon!* An early Roger Moore TV series
TEMPO	Upbeat or downbeat, whatever your fancy
TENNESSEE	Horses and owners that know how to spell
TENNILLE	Alone rhymes with a schlemiel . . . paired with the Captain, it still rhymes

TENNIS ANYONE	A tennis fanatic's pet
TENNYSON	A literary pet
TENOR	Heavyset male dogs with large egos
TEOK FU	Chinese shar-pei
TERENCE	A stamp collector's pet
TERESA	Animal with a halo
TERIYAKI	For a saucy pet
TERKEL	For a Stud
TERMINATOR	German shepherds, Doberman pinschers and pit bulls
TERRA-COTTA	An animal to match your kitchen floor
TERRY	Shaggy coats . . . Samoyeds, Angoras
TESIA	Golden Persians
TESLA	An underappreciated inventor (1856–1943)
TESSIE	Looks like your great-aunt
TEST PILOT	Must look good with helmet and goggles
TETHYS	Goddess of the sea . . . best fish in the tank
TEX	Largest example of its species
TEXAS RANGER	Guard dogs
TEXTBOOK	A perfect example of its breed
THACKERAY	English writer . . . wonderful pet name
THADDAEUS	Apostle, also known as St. Jude . . . also a wonderful pet name
THAI	A pet from Thailand
THALASSA	Pretentious name for a fish
THALBERG	Movie executive (1899–1936)
THALIA	Muse of comedy and poetry . . . one of the three graces
THANK-YOU	Will establish a slightly formal but loyal relationship
THARP	Either you're partial to the dancer or you have a lisp
THATCHER	English bulldogs, mastiffs

THAXTER	Great name for a male pet
THE BIG O	Oscar Robertson . . . basketball
THE GRADUATE	A Mrs. Robinson's pet
THE GREAT ONE	Wayne Gretzky . . . hockey
THE ROCKET	Raghib Ismale . . . football
THE RUSSIAN ROCKET	Pavel Bure . . . hockey
THE ULTIMATE WARRIOR	Wrestler
THE WORM	Dennis Rodman . . . basketball
THELMA	Neater than Louise
THEO	Van Gogh's brother. Ears intact
THEODORABLE	It's too adorable
THEODORAKIS	It's too ridiculous
THEODORE	Fabulous name
THEORY	Explains your crossbreed
THERAPY	A good listener
THERMAL	Persians, Angoras, any warm, hairy animal
THERMOS	Reminds you of your lunchbox
THESEUS	Slayed the Minotaur
THESPIAN	One of you has a dramatic flair
THICK	A pet that has a dense coat
THIMBLE	For little, itty-bitty animals
THIN	Also doubles with Thick
THISBE	Ill-fated lover of Pyramus
THOMAS	Likes English muffins
THOMAS MAGNUM	Likes champagne with its English muffin
THOMPSON	Its father was Tom
THOR	Norse god of thunder . . . wonderful for the larger breeds
THORAZINE	You figured out why it's so calm all the time

THOREAU	Animals who take care of themselves
THORN	A pet you regret
THORNDIKE	Scholarly
THORNEY	The queen bee
THORNY	The worker bee
THRILLER	Eyes and teeth that glow in the dark
THROCKMORTON	The Great Gildersleeve
THUG	Tough and hairless . . . bulldogs or pugs or Chinese shar-peis
THUMBELINA	Fairy tales and Danny Kaye
THUMBTACK	Sharp teeth, sharp claws
THUMPER	A character from *Bambi.* For any rabbit, of course
THUNDER	My friend's Great Dane. Her brother was Lightning
THUNDERBIRD	Beautiful example of its species
THURBER	Any pet would be flattered
THURGOOD	An animal with courage
THURMAN	Basset hounds
THURMOND	Your pet hawk
THURSDAY	When all else fails, resort to the day you got it
THYME	Likes double entendre
TIARA	Cockatoos, cockatiels
TIBBETT	Hamsters, gerbils, etc.
TIBBI	The hamster, gerbil, etc.'s pet
TIBERIUS	Attack dogs, piranhas, moray eels
TICKET	Your entree
TIDBIT	An animal you'll never take seriously
TIDDLYWINKS	A whimsical name for a whimsical pet
TIEGS	Cover girl material
TIERNEY	My mother's favorite actress
TIFFANY	Thin and elegant
TIFFIN	Not so thin
TIFFY	Just plain fat

TIGER	Maybe it's the stripes, maybe the personality
TIGER LILY	As long as it's yellow
TIGGER	Cute & resembles a drawing of a little tiger
TILLIE	Tennessee treeing brindles
TIM	A pal
TIMBUCKTOO	Where Tim is from, or replaces the first Timbuck
TIME OUT	It's not just a name, it's a concept
TIMER	It wakes you up at the same time every morning
TIMEX	Gives a licking and keeps on ticking
TIMOTHY	For that formal relationship
TINA	Tough, sexy, slightly hoarse voice
TINKER	Likes to fix things
TINKER BELL	Peter Pan's fixer-upper
TINNIE	For a pet with a tin ear
TINY	Another for your Minis
TINY TIM	Your pet tramples through the tulips
TIOMKIN	For a Russian blue
TIPPERARY	Irish setters who've come a long way
TIPPI	For those who have a distinctive patch of color at the ends of paws, tails, etc. . . . and like Hitchcock
TIPPY	For those with the markings who never heard of Hitchcock
TISH	Captain of the cheerleaders
TISHA	Her real name
TITAN	Great Danes, Saint Bernards, bullmastiffs
TITANIA	A *Midsummer Night's Dream*
TITO	Independent Communist leader of Yugoslavia
TKO	Boxers
TOAST	For a pet that receives kudos often
TOASTER	The pet that gives kudos often

TOBAGO	An island pet
TOBIAS	Pyrenees mastiffs
TOBY	Perfect for those whose gender is difficult to determine
TODD	More unusual than Ted and once married to Elizabeth Taylor
TODDY	Saint Bernards
TOFFEE	Brown classic tabbies
TOKAY	Dessert wine
TOKYO	A Rose's pet
TOKYO ROSE	Doesn't speak well of your relationship
TOLEDO	Holy
TOLKIEN	For hobbits
TOLSTOY	For pets that are very long
TOM	Triple with Dick and Harry
TOM COLLINS	A good standby
TOM JONES	For a rather sloppy eater
TOM THUMB	Double-paw animals
TOMAHAWK	Cockatoos, cockatiels, Toucans, poodles with fancy cuts
TOMLIN	Parrots or mynah birds
TOMMY	WHO?
TONI	A female mobster's pet
TONTO	A loyal companion of few words
TONY	A male mobster's pet
TOODLES	A pet that's always taking off
TOODY	Muldoon's partner
TOOT	This is so cute. It would do for any pet
TOOTSIE	You were told it was female, but you were told wrong
TOP HAT	For pets with black-and-white tails
TOPAZ	Yellow eyes
TOPPER	My favorite TV show while growing up . . . Cosmo and the Kerbys
TOPSIE	Pulis with blond curly hair

TOPSY	Black curly hair—poodles or the Chinese crested dog . . . hairless except for a tuft of hair on top of its head
TORTELLINI	A tortoise
TORTONI	Bisque coloring
TORY	Because, try as you might, conservative doesn't work as a name
TOSCANINI	Italian conductor (1867–1957)
TOSHI	Shih Tzu
TOSHIYUKI	Japanese spaniel
TOTAL RECALL	Parrots or elephants
TOTER	You'll be carrying it everywhere
TOTO	For a pet that's left Kansas
TOUCHÉ	For a pet that's always one up on you
TOULOUSE	Animals whose body length is double the leg length . . . dachshunds
TOUPEE	For the Mexican hairless . . . hairless except for one tuft of hair on its head
TOY	The name of Zelda and F. Scott Fitzgerald's bloodhound
TOYNBEE	Toy anythings, poodles, etc.
TRACER	Bloodhounds
TRACKER	Setters, retrievers, spaniels
TRACY	Goes well with Hepburn
TRAINER	Jogging companions, or animals that have wheels in their cages
TRAMP	Either you like Disney or it stays out all night
TRANQUILIZER	For any pet that lowers your blood pressure
TRAPPER	For a *M*A*S*H* fan
TRAUB	For water spaniels
TRAVELER	Because you can't leave home without it
TRAVIS	A McGee's pet
TRAVOLTA	An animal who's made a comeback
TREACHER	Fish

TREETOP	For those who don't live on the floor
TREKKER	See Doubles . . . Star
TRENT	A singer's pet
TREVOR	Old English sheepdogs, English mastiffs
TRIBUTE	An animal that was given as a gift
TRICK OR TREAT	Raccoons
TRICKY DICK	Companion to Checkers
TRIGÈRE	A designer's pet
TRIGGER	Horses
TRIGGER HAPPY	How Roy Rogers felt every time he saw his horse
TRINI	Cute and rhythmic
TRINIDAD	You like vacationing there
TRIPP	A third-generation nickname
TRIPPER	For a clumsy pet
TRISTAN	My friend Joy's horse
TRISTAR	White, wings, with a mane
TRIVIAL PURSUIT	A gerbil on its wheel
TROMBONE	Dachshunds
TROOPER	Your long walk companion
TROTSKY	Stay out of Mexico
TROUBLE	Guard dogs
TROY	Horses and Great Danes
TROYANOS	Canaries
TRUCKER	Bulldogs
TRUCK STOP	A bulldog's home
TRUDEAU	A Canadian Mounty's mount
TRUE	You have your doubts 'cause it's always a complicated story
TRUE BLUE	You have a very devoted pet
TRUFFAUT	For the French poodle kept in puffy haircuts
TRUFFLES	A very chichi pet

TRUJILLO	For a pet that takes over the house
TRUMAIN	For a pet that's truly from New England
TRUMAN	A pet you never expected to keep
TRUMBULL	For an English mastiff . . . big and majestic
TRUMP	For a bridge player
TRUMPET	Parrots
TSAR	Russian wolfhounds
TSARINA	Borzois
TSETSE	Small, pesky animals
TUBBS	Pair with Sonny Crockett
TUCCI	Italian pointers
TUCKER	For a pet that tires you out
TUCKET	Nan's pet
TUCSON	Reptiles
TUESDAY	A sexy pet
TUFF STUFF	An ironic choice. The animal isn't what it thinks it is
TUFFY	Bichon frises
TUGBOAT	The fat fish in the aquarium
TUGS	For a big dog that hasn't been leash trained
TUILERIES	French bulldogs
TULIP	For a pet that walks on its tiptoes
TUNER	Canaries
TUNNEY	Boxers
TUPPIE	A Tupperware salesman's pet
TURBO	Strong, powerful dogs
TURK	A tough animal . . . bulldogs, pit bulls, Maine coons
TURNER	Mastiffs
TURNIP	A very affectionate name
TURTLENECK	Chinese shar-peis, pugs, turtles

TUSHA	Was my Lhasa Apso, who turned nasty and tried to bite everyone . . . including me
TUSHINGHAM	Green-eyed, big rump
TUSSAUD	For a waxy pet
TUTSI	For a pet from Central Africa
TUTTI-FRUTTI	Mixed breeds
TUTU	Light on their feet. Birds
TUX	Black-and-whites
TV	This pet is good company, but you'll always feel a little guilty about it
TWAIN	Great pseudonym
TWANEY	What Twain's wife would call him
TWEED	English setters, certain calicos
TWEETY	Betrays a lack of imagination
TWEETY BIRD	Sylvester the cat's nemesis
TWIGGS	For a very thin pet
TWIGGY	Greyhounds, salukis
TWILIGHT	Russian blues, silver or blue Persians
TWINKIE	The dessert of choice in the '50s and '60s
TWINKLE	How I wonder where you are
TWITTY	Conway's pet
TWYLA	A dancer's pet
TYLER	Tippecanoe and . . . any of the water spaniels
TYNE E	Any of the minis
TYSON	For a pet that can impose its size
TZARKESH	A Russian blue

UBU	That dog at the end of certain TV programs
UDALL	For a basset hound . . . low to the ground and slow
UFFIZI	You love the gallery
UFO	It's a bit spacey
UGANDA	Rhodesian ridgebacks
UGGAMS	An entertaining small Continental spaniel
ULLMAN	For a pet that will ultimately Liv
ULRICH	German shorthairs
ULTIMA	Your pet wears makeup
ULTIMATE	The best pet
ULTRA	The even better pet
ULTRASONIC	Very fast pets
ULYSSES	Your pet has a middle initial (Preferably S)
UMAR	Iceland dogs
UMBER	Shorthair exotic shaded golds
UMBERTO	Italian hounds

UMBRELLA	You got it on a rainy day
UMP	For a baseball fan
UMPIRE	It will be the family mediator
UNCLE	A pet that can pin you down
UNCLE BEN	You love rice
UNCLE REMUS	A pet that likes to tell stories
UNCLE SAM	A patriot's pet
UNCONSCIOUS	Any lethargic pet
UNDERCOVER	A spy's pet
UNDERDOG	You love the cartoon
UNDERFOOT	You keep tripping over it
UNDERGROUND	A pet that shows resistance
UNDERWOOD	A typist's pet
UNGARO	A designing pet
UNGER	For a very, very, neat pet
UNION	For a pet of mixed parentage
UNION JACK	Another choice name for the Jack Russell terrier
UNITY	A peacekeeper
UNSER	Any pet that likes to race
UPBEAT	A happy pet
UPDATE	For an aspiring newscaster
UPDIKE	For an aspiring writer
UPHILL	For an aspiring skier
UPI	For an aspiring journalist
UPKEEP	It will need to go to the groomer more than once a month
UPROAR	A pet that causes pandemonium
UPSHOT	For a basketball fan
UPSTART	A rascal
UPTIGHT	A nervous, anxious pet
URANUS	A stargazer's pet
URBAN	A city pet living in the country
UREY	A cat with nine lives
URIAH	For a heap of a pet

URIS	A very prolific pet with a penchant for description
URSA	Swedish elkhounds
URSI	A friend who moved back to Switzerland
URSULA	I always think of Andress
USHER	The male dog that greets you at the door
USHERETTE	The female dog that greets you at the door
USTINOV	I always think of Peter
USURPER	It will take over the house
UTAH	You've always wanted to go west
UTOO	It always wants to be included
UTOPIA	The ideal pet
UTRILLO	A painter's pet
UZI	For a riveting pet

VACCARO	For a slightly plump but ever exciting pet
VACUUM	Your pet devours anything that falls to the ground
VADIM	For a Roger
VAGABOND	Your pet wanders from place to place
VAIL	A West Coast skier's pet
VALDEZ	You want it to serve as a reminder
VALENTINE	You liked *Scruples*
VALENTINO	For someone that likes either dressing well or old movies
VALENZUELA	Oh, Donna
VALIANT	Another Plymouth that bit the dust or you have an extremely brave pet
VALIUM	You have the ultimately relaxed pet
VALLEE	Not *How Green Was My . . .* but Rudy
VALLI	The Russian form of Vallee
VALLORIE	French pets
VAMP	Any pet that gets around
VAN	Standard schnauzers, Dutch border collies

VAN CLIBURN	For someone into music
VANDYKE	For someone into pointy beards
VAN GOGH	For someone into art and ears
VAN HEUSEN	For someone into shirts
VANCE	For someone into politics
VANCOUVER	For someone into dams
VANDERBILT	For someone into Gloria
VANESSA	For someone into Miss America politics
VANILLA	For someone also into music or ice cream . . . any white pet
VANITY	Again, music
VANNA	For someone into letters
VANNA BROWN	For a longhaired brown tabby
VANNA WHITE	For a longhaired white tabby
VARGAS	For a pinup pet
VASCO	Da Gama made an impression on you
VASILY	Artist's pet
VASSA	German longhaired pointers that can't say 'water' correctly
VAUDEVILLE	A pet for someone who remembers before 1930
VAUGHN	Ilia Kuriakian's partner
VEGA	For someone into Chevys
VEGAS	For someone into gambling
VELÁSQUEZ	For someone into history
VELVET	For someone blue
VENICE	For a water dog
VENUS	For someone into unattainable beauty
VENUS DE MILO	The formal name
VERA	My oldest friend Eva's sister. Or, pair with Norm
VERDI	For someone into music
VERDON	What you say when the whole family has finished dinner
VERMONT	An East Coast skier's pet

VERMOUTH	For someone into liquor
VERNE	American foxhounds
VERNON	An absolutely brilliant psychiatrist in Nashville, Tennessee
VERRAZANO	For someone into bridges
VERSAILLES	For someone into palaces
VERTIGO	For someone into heights
VESPER	For someone into prayer
VESPUCCI	For someone into history
VESTA	For someone into vests
VETERAN	For a pet that looks like it's been through the war
VICAR	For someone into Miss Marple stories
VICEROY	For someone from the '60s into smoking
VICHY	For someone into water
VICKI	For someone into Tiny Tim
VICKIE	Same pronunciation, different spelling
VICO	For someone into the Mafia
VICONT	For someone into titles
VICTOR	Pair with Victoria
VICTOR MATURE	You got an older pet whose name was Victor
VICTORIA	See Victor . . . you're not sure if it's a boy or girl
VICTORY	For someone into winning
VICTROLA	For someone into nostalgia
VIDA	For someone into life
VIDAL	For someone into hair
VIDEO	For someone into TV
VIDEO TAPE	For someone into production
VIDOR	For someone into foreign names
VIKING	For someone into gorgeous men
VILA	For someone into home repair
VILLA	For someone into the good life

VILLEROY	For someone into china
VINAIGRETTE	For someone into salad
VINCENT	What you call Vinny when you're mad at him
VINNY	Just one of the guys
VINTAGE	For a pet you plan to keep a long time
VINTON	Roses are red, my love
VIOLA	English cocker spaniels
VIOLET	Eva and Vera's mother
VIRGIL	Definitely for one of the American breeds . . . a serious and reliable pet
VIRGO	For someone into signs
VIRTUAL REALITY	A pet you only need to deal with when wearing your helmet
VISA	Your pet is getting you into debt
VISCOUNT	Westphalian bassets
VISCOUNTESS	Westphalian bassetesses
VISHNEVSKAYA	What a name. A borzoi or Russian wolfhound would be wonderful
VISITOR	You're not sure you want to keep the new pet
VISTA	Outdoor pets
VIVALDI	You love all four seasons
VIVIAN	Red Abyssinians
VIXEN	A pet you can't resist
VJ	You love music videos
VLADIMERE	Russian shorthairs, Russian blues, Moscows, Siberian huskies
VLADIMIR	Same pronunciation, different spelling
VODKA	It looks innocent enough!
VODKI	Vodka's pet name
VOGUE	For someone into sewing
VOIGHT	For a midnight cowboy
VOIT	For a plain ol' cowboy

VOLARE	Nel blu di pinto del blu, feliche costare la su
VOLCKER	For an avid Fed watcher . . . pair with Greenspan
VOLGA	A river pet
VOLTA	Black Forest hounds
VOLTAIRE	You're into drama
VON ZELL	HARRY!! *The Burns and Allen Show*
VONCE	A rascal in Yiddish
VONNEGUT	For a pet that leans towards satire and black humor
VOODOO	Your pet is possessed
VOYAGER	A pet that never stays home
VREELAND	A Small spitz
VUITTON	For a French mastiff . . . with an initialed collar
VULCAN	For a Trekkie

W. C. FIELDS	For a pet with a big nose, rosy cheeks, and a slightly vulgar manner
WADDLER	Ducks, bulldogs, boxers
WADDY	For a cowboy fan
WADER	Portuguese water dogs, frogs, turtles
WADSWORTH	For a long fellow . . . wirehaired dachshunds, Great Danes, snakes
WAFFLE	Neither you nor your pet are good at decisions
WAFTER	For a pet with a strong gas problem
WAGER	A gambler's pet
WAGGER	A very happy puppy
WAGNALL	A funky pet
WAGNER	A composer's pet
WAGS	My friend Wendy had a beagle named Wags when we were young. Great name
WAGTAIL	Birds
WAH-WAH	A guitarist's pet
WAHOO	Fish
WAITER	You've got a penguin

WAITLIST	It was hard to get
WALDEN	Your pet will live by a pond
WALDO	A pet you keep having to look for
WALDORF	You love salad
WALKER	A pet for a man named Johnny
WALKING PAPERS	You got it with the divorce
WALL STREET	An investor's pet
WALLER	A fat pet
WALLFLOWER	The runt of the litter
WALLIS	A pet aspiring to the throne
WALLY	*Leave It to Beaver*
WALNUT	Small brown pet
WALPOLE	Lapphunds . . . a Swedish dog, affectionate with children and distrustful of strangers
WALT	Good all-around name
WALTER	Another of my favorite names for a pet
WALTER BROWN	Any of the brown pets
WALTER MITTY	Your pet is a daydreamer
WALTON	You still enjoy watching the *Waltons*
WALTZ	You take dancing lessons
WAMBAUGH	A storyteller's pet
WANAMAKER	A clothes horse
WANDA	A FISH!!
WANDERER	For a pet that won't stay put
WAR HAWK	For any of your guard dogs, macaws, crows, Blue-fronted Amazons
WARD	Another nickname for Howard
WARDEN	Another one for guard dogs
WARFIELD	Yugoslavian tricolor hounds
WARHOL	Your pet likes canned food
WARING	For a mutt . . . as in blended
WARLOCK	Black cats

WARM UP	A jogger's pet
WARMONGER	Dobermans, pit bulls, boxers
WARNER	The first boy that ever told me I was pretty (see Mack the Knife)
WARPATH	My parents, when I told them
WARREN	American foxhounds
WARRIOR	Tawny Great Danes, or any of the larger breeds
WART	You loved *Camelot*
WARWICK	You're into the psychic world
WASHINGTON	You have political aspirations
WASSAIL	For people that drink to your health
WATCHDOG	The yappier small dogs
WATCHER	From the book of the same name, it would have to be a golden retriever
WATER BOY	You're planning to take it to all your games
WATERBERRY	Any of the water spaniels, fish, turtles, etc.
WATERGATE	For someone partial to the Nixon years . . . or not
WATERPROOF	Ducks or fish
WATERS	For any of the retrievers
WATSON	Pair with Holmes
WATTS	For a California type
WATUSI	You were a teenager in the '60s
WAVE DANCER	Brown California spangleds
WAVY	For a dog with curls—pulis, poodles, etc.
WAXY	For a pet that looks like it just got waxed—any of the hairless breeds
WAYNE	John
WEATHERMAN	Your pet refuses to go out when it's raining
WEAVER	Dennis or Sigourney fans
WEBER	You love to grill or you have a duck
WEBSTER	A good speller's pet

WEDGEWOOD	For a very delicate pet
WEDNESDAY	It was born on a Wednesday
WEEKENDER	You have joint custody of the pet as well as the kids . . . it goes when they go
WEEPER	For any pet that drools excessively
WEEZER	Good for a pug, for obvious reasons
WEEZIE	His nickname
WEIGHTLESS	An astronaut's pet
WEINER	Dachshunds, snakes
WELBY	You always wanted a doctor in the family
WELCH	Welsh corgis
WELCOME	Rottweilers (ha-ha)
WELFARE	Your pet is always begging
WELK	For a man whose name is Lawrence
WELLBUTRIN	You got it 'cause you were depressed
WELLER	For a pet that looks for wells
WELLINGTON	For a pet that likes walking in the rain or who wears boots
WELTY	For a person allergic to their cat or a Eudora fan
WEMBLEY	Brittany spaniels
WENCESLAS	See Good King
WENDEL	English setters
WENDOVER	Sussex spaniels
WENDY	A *Peter Pan* character
WENTWORTH	The first female pro golfer to win over $1M
WERTMULLER	A pet for an aspiring female director
WESLEY	Blue and white Scottish folds
WESTBERRY	A pet from Long Island
WESTBURY	A town in Long Island
WESTERN	You don't like to ride Eastern
WESTHEIMER	Your pet knows everything there is to know about sex

WESTIE	For a Western pet
WESTINGHOUSE	Your pet lights up your life
WESTMORELAND	Your pet likes to take command
WESTON	You're partial to the Boston suburb
WET BLANKET	For a pet that doesn't travel well
WHARTENBY	Longhaired Saint Bernards, Old English sheepdogs, bloodhounds
WHARTON	For a family with aspirations for its child to go to business school
WHATEVER	For someone very laid-back. Also, perfect for the mixed breed
WHEATCAKE	Another for the wheaton terrier
WHEATLY	My friend's soft-coated wheaton terrier
WHEATON	It used to be a very popular college
WHEELER DEALER	A used car salesman's pet
WHEELIE	You're going to train it to ride a bike
WHEEZIE	My friend Christopher's nickname
WHIG	The party running against Martin Van Buren in 1836. They lost
WHIMSY	My friend Penny's miniature poodle
WHISKERS	Cats
WHISKEY	Same as Brandy, everyone is into liquor names
WHISTLER	As long as it's a mother
WHISTLER'S MOTHER	Your pet sits all day
WHITEBREAD	White Manx, rabbits
WHITE CASTLE	Your pet will only eat square food
WHITE CHOCOLATE	Black and White American longhairs
WHITE FOOT	It has a white foot
WHITE GOLD	It doesn't want to be flashy
WHITE HALL	For someone into British politics
WHITE HOUSE	For someone into American politics
WHITE RUSSIAN	For someone into Russian politics

WHITE SOCKS	For someone into baseball politics
WHITIE	You drive a Ford and have a white pet
WHITMAN	It likes to sample
WHITNEY	It came from Houston
WHIZ KID	For a pet very easy to train
WHIZZER	Definitely for a male animal
WHO DUN IT	For mystery fans
WHO LOVES YOU	For Telly Savalas fans
WHOLE WHEAT	Another good name for a wheaton terrier
WHOLESALE	A shopper's pet
WHOLESALER	A pet that sells to the trade only
WHOOPIE	A happy pet
WHOPPER	A big pet
WHYLE	Boxers, parrots
WICKED WITCH	It refuses to be housetrained
WIDMARK	For a Richard fan
WIENER SCHNITZEL	Dachshunds, snakes
WIGGLES	Worms, snakes
WIG WAM	Your pet will live outdoors
WILLARD	Your pet can tell the weather
WILBUR	The pig in *Charlotte's Web*
WILCOX	For any of your English breeds
WILD BILL	See Bill Hickok
WILD RICE	A cook's pet
WILD THING	It makes your heart sing
WILDBERRY	Ruddy wild Abyssinians, wildebeests
WILDCAT	If you've got it, you'll know it
WILDE	You like Oscar
WILDER	For someone who likes Gene or Laura Ingalls
WILDFIRE	For any animal that produces copiously and often

WILDFLOWER	Blue silver patched tabby Maine coons, mutts
WILEY	A very clever pet
WILHELM	Any of the German breeds
WILKIE	A failed presidential candidate. Pair with Stevenson
WILKINS	Any of the English breeds
WILLFUL	For a pet that's hard to train
WILLIAM	For an heir to the throne
WILLIAMS	For the butler of the heir to the throne
WILLIE	Non-pedigree cats, dogs, turtles, birds
WILLIE WONKA	You know, the chocolate factory . . . perfect for a dark brown pet
WILLIS	BRUCE!
WILLOW	Blue-cream point Himalayans, anything feminine and wispy
WILLOW BREEZE	For a blue-cream point Himalayan that likes to go outdoors
WILLY	For a free pet
WILMA	Fred's wife in *The Flintstones*
WILSHIRE	It's your landmark when you go to Los Angeles
WILSON	Dennis the Menace's neighbor
WILT	You have a very tall pet
WILTON	How you feel standing next to that very tall pet
WIMBLEDON	For an avid tennis aficionado
WIMPIE	A meek pet
WINCHELL	Walter
WINCHESTER	You're either religious or into guns
WINDJAMMER	A sailor's pet
WINDSOR	For someone in the tie business
WINDY	For a pet with a lot of gas
WINEFRED	I love this. Just about any female would be gorgeous with this name

WINFREY	For a devoted Oprah fan
WINGER	Birds
WINGS	Also for birds
WINK	The cat that swallowed the canary
WINKLER	Very cute. As is Henry
WINNEDOO	Blue mitted ragdolls
WINNIE	For a Pooh
WINONA	For someone who likes horses
WINSTON	My cousin Frank's middle name
WINTHROP	This is a wonderful male name. Just imagine having both Winefred and Winthrop (maybe it's too much)
WIPEOUT	A surfer's pet
WIPPLE	Either you or your pet are into toilet paper
WIRETAP	A detective's pet
WISDOM	A dentist's pet
WISE GUY	A mobster's pet
WISECRACK	A comedian's pet
WISENHEIMER	Your pet is too smart for its own good
WISTERIA	A gardener's pet
WITHERS	A bad gardener's pet
WITHHOLDER	For a very independent cat
WITNESS	For a pet that sleeps on your bed
WITTIER	It thinks it's very funny
WIZARD	A genius pet
WOLFE	Yorkshire terriers
WOLFGANG	German shepherds
WOLFMAN	A name for a Jack Russell terrier
WONDER	For a pet that's a little out of it
WONDER BREAD	For a white fluffy pet
WONG	For someone who's never right
WOODBURY	For a common pet (I believe that only New Yorkers will get it)

WOODROW	For a Wilson fan
WOODSON	Redtick coonhounds
WOODSTOCK	Snoopy's bird
WOODWARD	A journalist's pet
WOODY	Woodpeckers
WOOFER	Basenjis (don't bark)
WOOFSTOCK	For a Basenji breeder
WOOLLY	Sheep
WOOLWORTH	A cheap sheep
WORDSWORTH	Parrots, macaws, mynahs
WORTH AVE.	For someone who likes to be reminded of the good life and Florida
WRANGLER	Good for a Jack Russell . . . or someone who lives in jeans
WRECKER	Also good for a Jack Russell
WRESTLE MANIA	Your ten-year-old loves it
WRINKLER	Chinese shar-pei
WRINKLES	Chinese shar-pei . . . again
WRITE OFF	An accountant's pet
WUNDERKIND	A parrot with an incredible vocabulary
WUZZIE	For a Devon rex . . . 'cause, he wasn't fuzzy, wuz he?
WYATT	For a person who longs to go west
WYATT EARP	For a pet that's quick on the draw
WYCLIFF	What you ask your dog Cliff after an accident
WYLER	Gordon setters
WYMAN	Brown classic tortie American curls
WYNETTE	Tennessee treeing brindles
WYNTER	Siberian huskies
WYOMING	Horses

X-MAN	Heroic with its own sense of reality
X-RATED	Manx, Japanese bobtails (tailless varieties)
X-RAY	Black-and-white calicos or animals caught in headlights
XANADU	For an animal that resembles Olivia Newton-John
XAVIER	For anyone into big bands, dancing, and swanky dinners
XENIA	Daughter in Mussorgsky's *Boris Godunov*
XENON	A colorless animal whose presence is barely felt
XENOPHON	Greek historian, disciple of Socrates
XEROX	Siamese twins or copy cats
XERXES	Persians
XIA	Chow Chows, Chinese crested dogs, Shih Tzus

XL   Though an excellent example of its
                     breed, it still can't spell

XMAS   Sled dogs with red noses

XYLOPHONE   A group of singing canaries. Individually
                     identified by note

YA TIDDLE	Thick necks
YAAKOV	Borzois, Russian blues
YACHTSMAN	Expensive fish
YACKER	Parrots, macaws
YAEL	For a serious, studious pet
YAGI	Baby talk. Save it for small, slightly misbehaving pets
YAGO	Your pet likes sangria
YAKITORI	Your pet likes Japanese food
YALE	Makes you the show-off
YAM	Orange-colored animals
YANA	The iguana
YANCY	Derringer. Cowboy country
YANG	Any Asian breed . . . Chow Chows, Shih Tzus, etc.
YANGTZE	You have three Asian breeds . . . Yang A and Yang B
YANKEE	American bred, particularly dogs who run after your car till you have to stop and order them home

**YANKEE
DOODLE**   Your pet resembles James Cagney

YANNI   Songbirds

YAPHE   Pronounced Ya-feh . . . means 'pretty' in
                   Hebrew

YAQUI   Another one for parrots and macaws

YARBOROUGH   For experienced bridge players

YARD MASTER   A successfully housebroken suburban
                   pet

YARDLEY   A clean, fresh-smelling pet that lives
                   outdoors

YARDSTICK   A dressmaker's pet . . . also good for
                   dachshunds

YARMULKE   Has a dark patch on top of its head

YARNIE   Tall tailed pets

YARROW   Any yellow animal

YASAHIRO   Japanese Bobtails, Akitas, Japanese
                   Spaniels

YASMIN   Persians

YASSER   For a pharaoh dog . . . or a real mutt

YASTRZEMSKI   Boston terriers. Nickname Yaz

YATES   You have a poetic streak, you just can't
                   spell

YAZ   See Yastrzemski

YEASTY   Chameleons and fish

YEATS   Poet

YEHUDA   For a religious pet

YELLER   It's sort of like Lassie is to a collie . . .
                   Yeller is to an old yellow Lab . . . also
                   good for a loud parrot

YELLOW BELLY   Appropriate for a variety of birds. Also
                   to spooked cats and neurotic dogs

YELLOWSTONE   Reptiles

YELTSIN   Siberian huskies, Russian wolfhounds,
                   Afghans, borzois

YEOMAN   Working English setters

YEOMAN OF THE GUARD	Dobermans, German shepherds, etc.
YERTLE	The turtle
YES	For a basketball fan
YESTERDAY	Pet beetles
YEVTUSHENKO	See Yeltsin . . . any of the Russian breeds
YIDDISH	A particularly expressive parrot
YIN	The female half of a Chow Chow pair
YIPPIE	Coat looks tie-dyed
YITZHAK	Begins as a rebel, ends as a leader
YMCA	Any pet that knows how to move its arms to make the letters of the song
YO	A very cool pet
YO-YO	A not so cool pet
YODA	A pug would be perfect, or a bulldog
YODEL	A singing canary
YODELS	A chorus of singing canaries
YOGA	For a very quiet, agile pet
YOGI	For a very quiet, agile pet who looks good in white
YOGI BEAR	A large example of Yogi . . . or its complete opposite
YOGURT	Vegetarian pets with no dairy allergies
YOKE	Birds, snakes, or oxen
YOKO	Japanese bobtails
YOLANDA	Parrots, macaws, talkative animals
YONA	For a lazy pet . . . it just sounds like a lazy name . . . sort of like 'yawn'
YOO HOO	Chocolate Labs, chocolate point Siamese
YORBA	The Great . . . though, not as great as Zorba
YORK	Yorkshire terriers
YORKE	Not just any Yorkshire Terrier

YORTY	Suggests a nickname for a longer version that's been in the family for five generations
YOSEMITE	Reptiles
YOUCON	Toucans
YOUNG	For a pet that thinks it's Father Knows Best
YOUNGMAN	For a pet that thinks it's a comedian
YOYO	Pet frogs
YUBA	Snakes, frogs, lizards, and pigs
YUCATAN	Chihuahuas, Mexican hairless
YUCHI	For tiny, cute, affectionate lap sitters
YUKI	Though you love it, it does some disgusting things
YUKON	For Alaskan malamutes, Eskimo dogs
YUKON KING	From the 1950s TV show . . . he was a husky
YUL	Anything hairless
YULE	It was a Christmas present
YUM YUM	You have a very good-looking pet
YUPPIE	A pet with a Rolex and a Land Rover
YURI	The Russian breeds again
YUSEF	Songbirds with jazz repertoire
YVETTE	Sexy with heavy eyeliner markings
YVONNE	A more mature sexuality

ZABAGLIONE	Cream color pets . . . something all whipped up like a bichon frise
ZABAR	For a pet that lives in New York and likes good deli food
ZABRISKIE	Pointers
ZACCHEUS	Sounds biblical, but probably isn't
ZACH	A short pet, or a pet with a short attention span
ZACHARIAS	An Old Testament animal
ZACHARY	A twentieth-century animal
ZADIE	Means 'grandpa' in Yiddish
ZADOK	Pair with Medoc
ZADORA	Sexy, pouty, passable voice
ZAFTIG	Any pet with an ample figure
ZAHIR	For any pet that likes heat
ZAKAIAH	Goes well with Jebediah and Obediah
ZAKI	My uncle up in Boston
ZALMAN	Fish
ZAMBONI	Huskies
ZANE	Horses

ZANE GRAY	Gray horses . . . old enough to remember the Zane Gray Theater?
ZANG	Song birds with German accents
ZANUCK	A pet into old movies
ZANY	For the pet that makes you laugh
ZANZA	Any particularly foreign and strong-looking pet
ZANZIBAR	Poicephalus parrots, African Greg parrots
ZAPATA	A pet that every time you look at him you want to yell . . . VIVA Zapata!
ZAPPA	Long, scraggly hair, funny, irreverent
ZAPPER	It replaces your remote control
ZAPPI	Attack dogs. The 'i' is disarming and will catch attackers off guard
ZARA	For any of the female Russian breeds, though historically appropriate for dalmatians
ZAW	The macaw
ZAZEN	Meditation in Zen Buddhism. Use it on a turtle to explain what goes on inside that shell
ZAZI	Female French poodles
ZASU	Pitts . . . *My Little Margie*
ZEALOT	A pet that guards its toys, food, children, and owner's children very well
ZECH	Zecharia's nickname
ZECHARIA	A twist on Zacharias
ZEE ZEE	For your smaller breeds
ZEFF	You already used up Jeff, Heff, and Ref
ZEFFER	The full name
ZEFFIRELLI	Italian stage and screen director
ZEISS	Cats with extraordinary vision
ZEITGEIST	Any pet that's the current rage
ZELDA	You can go two ways . . . anything with a twitchy nose (Dobie Gillis) or F. Scott's match

ZELIG	Chameleons with glasses
ZELLA	Reminds you of a cheap wine
ZELLE	Female French poodles
ZEN	See Zazen
ZENA	I believe that Zena Bethume played a nurse on TV in the '60s
ZENITH	For a couch potato . . . or the top of its breed
ZENOBIA	Shelled pets . . . turtles
ZEPH	Zephan's nickname
ZEPHAN	A Russian Stephen
ZEPHANIAH	For a Russian blue or borzoi
ZEPHYR	A bird from the West
ZEPHYRUS	A bird that acts like it's from the West
ZEPPELIN	A bird that's lost the ability to fly
ZERBE	Greek pets
ZERLINA	Character in Mozart's *Don Giovanni*
ZERO	Dalmatians
ZESTA	A happy-go-lucky pet that makes the most of life
ZESTY	Not exactly lusty, peppy, or zippy—sort of a combination
ZETTA	Not quite as active as Zesta and Zesty
ZEUS	An animal of the highest authority
ZEZE	To be said in a high voice
ZHUKOV	A KGB sounding name . . . Russian wolfhound, Samoyed, Karelian bear dog
ZIA	Makes me think of a Chia Pet . . . just water it and the hair keeps growing
ZIEGFELD	A pet that is either a folly or a great dancer
ZIFFI	A made-up name whose rhyme with 'iffy' is not coincidental
ZIGZAG	Tabbies, mice
ZIGGY	Of cartoon fame
ZILCH	A pet you don't expect anything from

ZILLION	Insect collection
ZIMBALIST	Stephanie for the '90s . . . Efrem for the '60s, '70s, and '80s
ZIMMI	When you want the name to be a bit more exotic than Jimmy
ZINC	Blue point Balinese, Blue point Birman, Cornish rex, silver Persian, etc.
ZINCKY	Zinc's nickname
ZINDEL	A spinster pet
ZINFANDEL	A wine lover's pet
ZING	Birds with irritating high-pitched voices
ZINGER	Hits its target every time
ZINNIA	Yet another flower to add to the list . . . triple with Lily and Petunia
ZIPCODE	Homing pigeons or a postman's pet
ZIPLOCK	A pet that doesn't know when to keep quiet
ZIPPER	A pet that does know when to keep quiet
ZIRCON	Fake but fairly convincing pedigree
ZIRCONIA	Same as above
ZITHER	Songbirds
ZITI	Snakes, dachshunds . . . tubular pets
ZIV	My friend's big bear of a brother in the restaurant business
ZIZI	A very endearing pet name
ZODIAC	Fish (or Rams, Bulls, Crabs, Lions, etc.)
ZOE	My sister-in-law's mixed breed
ZOISIA	A pet that loves to roll in the grass
ZOLA	Any of the French breeds
ZOLTAN	Powerful name. Good for a Great Dane or Borzoi or anything big
ZOMBIE	Snake god of voodoo cults (yuch, I thought it was just someone that couldn't get it together)

ZONA	French name for shingles . . . save it for pets with shells
ZONK	For heavy sleepers
ZONTIA	For a very big feline
ZOOM LENS	A photographer's pet
ZOOMER	Pet looking good in a helmet
ZOOT SUIT	Brightly colored fish
ZORA	A female Zorro-type
ZORBA	A pet with a lust for life
ZORI	Love means never having to say you're zori (Zori!)
ZORN	Sounds like a guard dog
ZOROASTER	Persians
ZORRO	My grandmother and I used to watch this together . . . any pet that looks like it wears a mask
ZOYA	Russian blues, Russian wolfhounds, etc.
ZSA ZSA	You own several sisters but have discarded all their mates
ZUBERRY	You're hoping that Ben & Jerry will name a flavor after it
ZUBIN	Give it a baton to go with its black tail
ZUBOV	A defensive pet that likes ice hockey
ZUCCHERO	A very popular Italian singer (pronounced 'zuckero')
ZUCCHETTO	What his mother calls him
ZUCCHINI	Snakes, iguanas, geckos
ZUCKER	For a sweet pet
ZUCKIE	An even sweeter pet
ZUKERMAN	For a sweet pet that looks like it's a businessman
ZUKOR	This sounds big, like a Rottweiler
ZULA	The first Abyssinian cat to reach England
ZULU	Dobermans, German shepherds, Rottweilers, etc.

ZUNI	This is good for any of the hunting dogs
ZUPER	You have an accent
ZUPPA INGLESE	One of my very favorite desserts
ZURIEL	Russian blues
ZUTZKA	Good for a smaller breed, like a cairn terrier, miniature poodle, Jack Russell terrier
ZUZI	Shih Tzus, Lhasa Apsos, Persians or Egyptian Maus
ZUZUSHII	For a very fast raw fish
ZVENGAHLI	An older pet you're still breeding
ZWEIG	For a pet that can drink from a flask
ZWIEBACK	Your pet likes the cookies as much as your baby does
ZWINDLER	For a pet that competes with your baby for the cookies
ZWING	You still have the accent

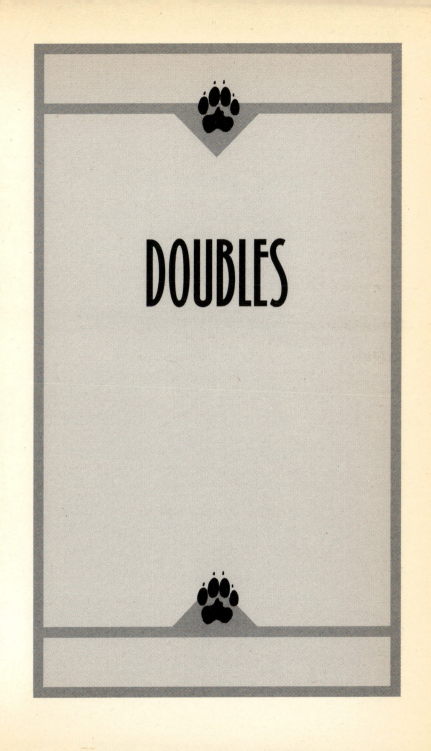

DOUBLES

DOUBLES

Abbott & Costello

Abercrombie & Fitch

Adonis & Venus

Alice & Ralph

Alvin & Alley

AM & FM

Amos & Andy

Annette & Fabian

Annie Oakley &
Buffalo Bill

Antony & Cleopatra

Arafat & Gaza Stripper

Archie & Betty

Archie & Edith

Archie & Jughead

Ari & Jackie

Arsenic & Old Lace

Astair & Rogers

Aurora & Borealis

Babbitt & Myrna

Babe & Ruth

Bach & Beethoven

Bacon & Eggs

Bambi & Thumper

Bardot & Vadim

Barney & Betty

Barney & Fred

Barnum & Bailey

Batman & Catwoman

Batman & Robin

Beaver & Wally

Beezus & Henry

Beezus & Ramona

Ben & Jerry

Bert & Ernie

Bert & Nan

Betamax & VHS

Beulah & Hazel

Bill & Hillary

Black & White

Blackjack & Roulette

Blondie & Dagwood

Blue & Chip

Bobby Darin &
Sandra Dee

Bogie & Bacall

Bolognese & Milanese

Bolshoi & Misha

Bonnie & Clyde

Bordeaux & Beaujolais

Boris & Bela

Boris & Karloff

Boris & Natasha

Bosley & Bri

Bourguignon & Bearnaise

Bow & Arrow

Brando & Bogart

Bri & Blue

Bride & Groom

Bridget & Bernie

Brigitte & Bardot

Brioche & Baguette

Bristol & Cream

Broadway &
Times Square

Brooks & Bancroft

Bruce & Demi

Bryant & Katie

Buckwheat & Alfalfa

Bunsen & Beeker

Burns & Allen

Buster & Brown

Caesar & Cleopatra

Cagney & Lacy

Cagney &
Yankee Doodle

Cain & Abel

Candide & Voltaire

Captain & Tenille

Carlo & Sophia

Carol & Clark

Carrot Cake &
Banana Bread

Carson & Letterman

Cassius Clay & Muhammad Ali

Catwoman & Bruce

Cha Cha & Rumba

Champagne & Caviar

Chanel & Arpege

Charles & Camella

Charles & Diana

Charley & Steinbeck

Charlie Chan & #1 Son

Chewbacca & C3PO

China & Porcelain

Chip & Dale

Churchill & Thatcher

Cinderella & Prince Charming

Clarabell & Chief Thunderthud

Clarabell & Howdy Doody

Clark & Lois

Coco & Chanel

Coke & Pepsi

Columbus & Isabella

Copa & Cabana

Cowboy & Indian

Cracker & Jack

Crimson & Clover

Crockett & Tubbs

Darryl & Strawberry

David & Goliath

Da Vinci & Leonardo

Day & Night

Democrat & Republican

DeNiro & Streep

Dennis & Mr. Wilson

DeVito & Schwarzenegger

Diana & Fergie

Diane & Carla

Diane & Frasier

Diane & Sam

Dick & Jane

Dick & Tracy

Dickens & Copperfield

Dijon & Honey

Disco & Rock 'N' Roll

DJ & CD

Don Quixote & Dulcinea

Donald & Goofy

Donna & Alex

Donna & Richie

Dorothy & Oz

Dorsey & Miller

Dow & Jones

Duke & Duchess

Duke Ellington &
Count Basie

Dwight & Mamie

Ebony & Ivory

Ed & Johnny

Ed & Ralph

Ed & Trixie

Either & Or

Eliza Doolittle &
Henry Higgins

Elliot & Ness

Eloise & Plaza

Elvis & Priscilla

F. Scott & Fitzgerald

Farrah & Ryan

Fay & Betinna

Ferdinand & Isabella

Fergie & Andrew

Fester & Lurch

Feta & Mozzarella

Fettuccine & Alfredo

Fibber McGee & Molly

Filo & Fax

Flash Gordon &
Buck Rogers

Frank & Kathie Lee

Frankie & Johnnie

Franklin & Eleanor

Frasier & Lilith

Fred & Ethel

Fred & Ginger

Freddie & Flossie

Freebie & Bean

Frick & Frack

Funicello & Avalon

Funk & Wagnall

Gabby Hayes &
Nelly Belly

Gable & Lombard

Garbo & Dietrich

Garfield & Odie

Gene Autry &
Gabby Hayes

George & Barbara

George & Gracie

George & Ira

Gidget & Moondoggie

Gilligan & Skipper

Gimbel's & Macy's

Gin & Tonic

Ginger & Mary Ann

Godfrey & Irene

Goldfinger & Bond

Goldie & Kurt

Gomez & Morticia

Gorbie & Brezhnev

Green Eggs & Ham

Griffin & Sabine

Groucho & Harpo

Gucci & Fendi

Gulliver & Yahoo

Guns & Roses

Haiku & Poetry

Hamlet & Laertes

Hamlet & Macbeth

Hamlet & Ophelia

Hans Brinker & Gretel

Hansel & Gretel

Harry & Leona

Harry & Winston

Harvard & Yale

Hawkeye & BJ

Hawkeye & Pierce

Hawn & Russell

Henny & Youngman

Henry & Ribsy

Hero & Leander

Hiawatha & Longfellow

Him & Her

Hodge & Podge

Holly Golightly & Cat

Holmes & Watson

Hook & Pan

Hope & Anchor

Hoss & Little Joe

Hot Fudge & Chocolate

Hot Lips & Frank

Howard & Robin

Howdy Doody &
Uncle Bob

Hugs & Kisses

Humphrey & Bette

Hunky & Dory

Huntley & Brinkley

Hurly & Burly

Ice Cream & Sprinkles

Ichabod & Crane

Ike & Mamie

Iliad & Odyssey

Ipso & Facto

Irma La & Douce

Ish & Kabibble

Ishmael & Moby Dick

J.R. & Bobby

Jack Benny & Rochester

Jacoby & Meyers

Jake & Ellwood

James Bond & Moneypenny

James Brown &
Stevie Wonder

Jean & Johnny

Jeeves & Bertie

Jekyll & Hyde

Jim & Margaret

Jim & Tammy

Jimmy & Mr. White

Joan & David

Joanie & Chachi

Joe & Frank

Joe Friday &
Bill Gannon

John & Jackie

John & Yoko

June & Ward

Karloff & Lugosi

Katherine & Spencer

Ken & Barbie

Kermit & Miss Piggy

KGB (Kaygee) & CIA (Ci)

King & Queen

King Arthur & Guinevere

King Arthur & Merlin

King Arthur &
Sir Lancelot

King Lear & Othello

Kipling & Kim

Klinger & Radar

Klink & Schultz

Kramden & Norton

Lady & Tramp

Lady Chatterley & Oliver

Lady Godiva &
Fanny Farmer

Lancelot & Guinevere

Laverne & Shirley

Lenny & Squiggy

Leno & Letterman

Lerner & Low

Lewis & Clark

Li'l Abner & Daisy May

Lincoln & Mercury

Linus & Lucy

Little Joe & Pa

Liz & Richard

Liz & Richard

Liz & Richard

Liz & Richard

Lois & Jimmy

Lone Ranger & Tonto

Lucy & Desi

Lucy & Ethel

Lucy & Ricky

Lugosi & Dracula

Luke & Laura

Luke & Princess Leia

Lyndon & Lady Bird

Lysander & Hermia

Macduff & Fife

Mackintosh & T.J.

Magoo & Backus

Major & Minor

Marcel & Marceau

Marcello & Sofia

Marcellus & Horatio

Marshal Dillon &
Miss Kitty

Max & Wild Thing

Maxwell Smart & 99

McGarret & Dan-O

McGillicudy & Ricardo

Meat & Potatoes

Melvin & Howard

Mercedes & Porsche

Mertz & Ricardo

Mickey & Minnie

Mikado & Pooh-Bah

Mildred & Elsie

Milly & Olly

Miss Marple & Poirot

Moe & Larry

Montague & Capulet

Mork & Mindy

Mozart & Tchaikovsky

Mrs. Robinson & Benjamin

Muhammad & Ali

Mutt & Jeff

My Man & Godfrey

Napoleon & Josephine

Nate & Al

Nick & Nora

Norm & Carla

Norton & Kramden

Norton & Trixie

O'Hara & Butler

O. Henry & Snickers

Oedipuss & Oedipup

Onyx & Coral

Oprah & Phil

Oscar & Emmy

Oscar & Felix

Oxford & Cambridge

Ozzie & Harriet

Pablo & Paloma

Parsley & Sage

Pat & Vanna

Peaches & Cream

Pebbles & Bamm Bamm

Peewee Reese &
Jackie Robinson

Penguin & Joker

Perry & Della

Peter & Captain Hook

Peter & Tinkerbell

Phil & Marlo

Phillip & Elizabeth

Phyllis & Fang

Pinkie & Lee

Pinocchio & Woody

Pirouette & Minuet

Pitter & Patter

Plain & Fancy

Popeye & Olive Oyl

Porgy & Bess

Porsche & Mercedes

Portnoy & Complaint

Preakness & Belmont

Preppie & Hippie

Prince & Princess

Prince Charming & Cinderella

Pulitzer & Nobel

Puss & Boots

Pyramus & Thisbe

Queen Anne &
King George

Ralph & Alice

Rather & Chung

Ravel & Bolero

Regis & Kathie Lee

Rhett & Scarlett

Rhoda & Phyllis

Rhythm & Blues

Rick & Casablanca

Riddler & King Tut

Ritz & Carlton

Ritz & Cracker

Rob & Laura

Robin Hood &
Maid Marian

Rock & Doris

Rock & Roll

Rocky & Adrian

Rocky & Bullwinkle

Rodgers & Hammerstein

Rodgers & Hart

Romeo & Juliet

Ronnie & Nancy

Rooney & Hardy

Rosalind & Jimmy

Rosemary & Baby

Rosemary & Thyme

Rough & Ready

Roy Rogers &
Dale Evans

Roy Rogers &
Gabby Hayes

Roy Rogers &
Gene Autry

Ruby & Sapphire

Rudolph & Santa

Rum & Coke

Salinger & Hemingway

Sally & Buddy

Salt & Peppa

Salt & Pepper

Salvador & Dali

Samson & Delilah

Schultzy & Bob

Scotch & Soda

Scott & Zelda

Shakespeare & Tennyson

Shari & Lambchop

Sheriff & Deputy

Sheriff & Miss Kitty

Sherlock & Hemlock

Silver & Trigger

Simon & Garfunkel

Sky King & Penny

Smith & Wesson

Snoopy & Linus

Snoopy & Woodstock

Socrates & Xanthippe

Sofia & Carlo

Soufflé & Mousse

Speedy & Alka-Seltzer

Spenser & Hawk

Spenser & Susan

Spin & Marty

Spock & Kirk

Star & Trekker

Starsky & Hutch

Sting & Axl

Stocks & Bonds

Stoli & Absolut

Sugar & Spice

Sullivan & Cromwell

Swash & Buckle

Sweet & Low

T. S. & Eliot

Taft & Hartley

Tempest & Teapot

The Donald & Marla

Thelma & Louise

Thick & Thin

Thurston Howell III & Lovey

Tiffany & Cartier

Tiger & Lily

Time & Newsweek

Timex & Bulova

Tin Man & Cowardly Lion

Tippecanoe & Tyler

Toast & Jelly

Tolkien & Hobbit

Tolstoy & Karenina

Tom & Jerry

Tonto & Lone Ranger

Toody & Muldoon

Track & Field

Tracy & Hepburn

Trinidad & Tobago

Trixie & Alice

Troilus & Cressida

Tunney & Dempsey

TV & Guide

Tweety & Sylvester

Uncle Tonoose & Danny

Valentine & Proteus

Venus & Eartha

Victor & Victoria

Vim & Vigor

Vinaigrette & Roquefort

Violet & Daisy

Vivaldi & Rachmaninoff

Wait & And See

Wendy & Nana

Willard & Mr. G.

Winfrey & Donahue

Winky Dink & You

Winwood & High Life

Wolf & Red Riding Hood

Yankee & Doodle

Zeus & Apollo

Zsa Zsa & Merv

TRIPLES

TRIPLES

A. J. Foyt	Unser	Andretti
ABC	NBC	CBS
Agassi	Borg	Stich
Alfred	Batman	Robin
Alto	Soprano	Tenor
Amos	Andy	Kingfish
Archie	Betty	Veronica
Archie	Betty	Jughead
Archie	Edith	Meathead
Ashe	Laver	Rosewall
Astro	Padre	Red
Bach	Beethoven	Ravel
Batman	Robin	Alfred
Batman	Catwoman	Vickie

Beaver	Wally	Eddie
Beezus	Ramona	Henry
Bell	Book	Candle
Bert	Ernie	Big Bird
Betty	Kathy	Bud
Betty	Barney	Bamm Bamm
Billy	Allison	Jane
Boogie	Lindy	Swing
Boris	Natasha	Badenov
Brandon	Dillon	Steve
Brandy	Whisky	Shotsie
Brewer	White Sock	Ranger
Brioche	Baguette	Croissant
Bryant	Katie	Willard
Buddy	Rob	Sally
Bullwinkle	Rocky	Dudley Do-Right
Cha Cha	Mambo	Rumba
Chanel	Arpége	Brute
Chanel	Borghese	Lancôme
Charles	Di	Camella
Chiffon	Organdy	Organza
Cinderella	Prince Charming	Slipper
Clarabell	Howdy Doody	Buffalo Bob
Cobb	Babe	Gehrig
Coco	Chanel	Paris
Colette	Yvette	Suzette

Colonel Klink	Lebeau	Schultz
Crosby	Stills	Nash
Democrat	Republican	Independent
Diane	Sam	Frasier
Dick	Jane	Spot
Dimaggio	Miller	Monroe
Dobie	Zelda	Gillis
Don Diego	Zorro	Mask
Donald	Hot Lips	Frank
Donna	Kelly	Brenda
Dorothy	Blanche	Rose
007	Goldfinger	Octapussy
Duchess	Duke	Count
Eat	Drink	Be Merry
F. Scott	Zelda	Fitzgerald
Fendi	Gucci	Mark Cross
Fergie	Andrew	Elizabeth
Feta	Mozarella	Brie
Frazier	Foreman	Ali
Fred	Ethel	Lucy
Friar Tuck	Maid Marian	Robin Hood
Gene Autry	Roy Rogers	Slim Pickens
George	Gracie	Harry Von Zelz
Giant	Dodger	Brave
Graf	Seles	Sabatini
Griffith	Joyner	Jackie
Groucho	Harpo	Zeppo

Guggenheim	Metropolitan	Frick
Gypsy	Rose	Lee
Hamburger	Hot Dog	Fries
Hamlet	Ophelia	Macbeth
Harpo	Groucho	Chico
Harvard	Yale	Princeton
Hawkeye	Hot Lips	Frank
Hawkeye	Pierce	Potter
Heart	Diamond	Spade
Hogan	Lebeau	Schultz
Hot Fudge	Chocolate	Sprinkles
Hot Lips	Frank	Klinger
Howard Stern	Robin	Stuttering John
Howdy Doody	Uncle Bob	Clarabell
Imelda	Manila	Pumps
Inkster	Cockerill	Mcgill
Jack	Benny	Rochester
Jane	Workout	Ted
Jim	Margaret	Betty
Jimmy	Lois	Clark
Joan	Jackie	Collins
John	Philip	Sousa
John	Paul	George
Joyner	Koch	Ivan
June	Ward	Beaver
Kentucky Derby	Preakness	Belmont
Kermit	Miss Piggy	Oscar

King	Queen	Jack
King	Prince	Princess
King	Queen	Duke
King	Court	Goolagong
King Arthur	Guinevere	Lancelot
Klinger	Radar	B.J.
Larry	Darryl	Darryl
Laverne	Shirley	Squiggie
Little Joe	Pa	Hoss
Liston	Tyson	Holyfield
Lois	Jimmy	Perry
Lone Ranger	Tonto	Silver
Lucy	Peanuts	Linus
Lucy	Sky	Diamonds
Lucy	Ricky	Fred
Manny	Moe	Jack
Mantle	Mays	Ruth
Marigold	Petunia	Pussy Willow
Mary	Phyllis	Rhoda
Mason	Street	Drake
Maybelline	Clinique	Revlon
McEnroe	Connors	Vilas
Mediterranean	Pacific	Atlantic
Mickey	Minnie	Donald Duck
Miss Lane	Mr. Kent	Mr. White
Miss Marple	Mrs. Fletcher	Poirot
Moe	Larry	Curly

Money Market	Mutual Fund	CD
Morticia	Gomez	Fester
Mr. White	Kent	Miss Lane
Muhammad Ali	Cassius Clay	Joe Foreman
Murphy	Corky	Frank
Navratilova	Evert	Austin
News	Weather	Traffic
Nick	Nora	Asta
Nicklaus	Player	Trevino
Nixon	Bush	Ford
Norm	Vera	Carla
Orantes	Newcombe	Nastase
Oriole	Red Sock	Indian
Ozzie	Harriet	Ricky
Pablo	Paloma	Picasso
Paul	Ringo	George
Peanuts	Popcorn	Cracker Jack
Pebbles	Wilma	Fred
Penguin	Joker	Robin
Penne	Macaroni	Ravioli
Perry	Della	Paul
Peter	Nana	Captain Hook
Peter Pan	Tinkerbell	Wendy
Petunia	Gardenia	Gladiola
Picasso	Matisse	Kandinsky
Pierce	B.J.	Potter
Pierre	Plaza	Regency

Plaza	Peninsula	St. Regis
Popeye	Olive Oyl	Sweet Pea
Porsche	Mercedes	Volkswagen
Prince	Head	Wilson
Private	Lieutenant	Colonel
Question	Period	Exclamation
Ralph	Lauren	Polo
Reebok	Fila	Nike
Rick	Ilsa	Casablanca
Ringo	Starr	Drummer
Rolex	Timex	Bulova
Roy	Dale	Trigger
Sampras	Edberg	Becker
Scarlett	Rhett	Ashley
Secretariat	Bold Forbes	Seattle Slew
Shakespeare	Macbeth	Portia
Sherlock	Dr. Watson	Holmes
Small	Medium	Large
Snap	Crackle	Pop
Snoopy	Woodstock	Lucy
Sonny	Crockett	Tubbs
Sony	Panasonic	Sharp
Soup	Sandwich	Dessert
Spaulding	Penn	Wilson
Spenser	Hawk	Susan
Spinks	Holmes	Norton

Stallone	Rocky	Rambo
Stengel	Hodges	Weaver
Stocks	Bonds	Treasuries
Summer	Spring	Autumn
Superman	Batman	Spiderman
Sweet	Low	Sugar
Tiffany	Cartier	Bulgari
Tin Man	Cowardly Lion	Wizard
Tom	Dick	Harry
Tunney	Dempsey	Sharkey
Uncle Tonoose	Danny	Rusty
Venus	Mars	Jupiter
Violet	Daisy	Lily
Washington	Lincoln	Roosevelt
Whole Wheat (Wheatly)	Rye	Pumpernickel
Woodstock	Linus	Lucy
Yankee	Giant	Met

THE 100 MOST POPULAR DOG NAMES IN NYC

RANK	MALE	FEMALE
1	Max	Princess
2	Rocky	Lady
3	Lucky	Sandy
4	Duke	Ginger
5	Prince*	Sheba
6	Rusty	Brandy
7	King	Muffin
8	Blackie	Samantha
9	Buddy	Missy
10	Brandy	Daisy
11	Benji*	Candy
12	Champ	Misty

*Indicates tied ranking with the next name

13	Sam	Cindy
14	Charlie	Pepper
15	Rex	Tiffany
16	Bandit	Penny
17	Smokey	Lucky
18	Teddy	Fluffy
19	Buster	Queenie
20	Sparky	Coco
21	Pepper	Cookie
22	Rambo	Bambi
23	Butch*	Heidi
24	Snoopy	Sasha
25	Spike	Duchess
26	Tiger	Tara
27	Fluffy*	Baby
28	Sandy	Gigi
29	Toby	Kelly
30	Bruno*	Buffy
31	Mickey	Maggie
32	Barney	Susie
33	Brownie	Shadow*
34	Gizmo*	Tasha
35	Shadow	Bonnie
36	Bear	Honey
37	Coco	Cleo

*Indicates tied ranking with the next name

38	Skippy	Sheena*
39	Samson	Tina
40	Scruffy	Lucy
41	Dusty	Mandy
42	Spanky	Molly
43	Casey	Holly
44	Pepe	Peaches
45	Jake	Crystal*
46	Baron	Taffy
47	Sammy	Trixie
48	Brutus	Pebbles
49	Muffin	Fifi*
50	Buttons	Gypsy

*Indicates tied ranking with the next name

MY FAVORITE
100
(or thereabouts)
NAMES

MY 100 FAVORITES

Alfred	Brando	Dudley
Amos	Brioche	Earl
Angus	Bubba	Edgar
Antoine	Byron	Edna
Apollo	Caesar	Ethel
Aristotle	Chanel	F. Scott
Armani	Cheyenne	Farrah
Axl	Cornelius	Frankie
Beans	Cyril	Frazier
Bing	Daisy	Freddy
Blossom	Dakota	Gabbi
Bo	Digger	Garbo
Bogie	Dillon	George

Goldie	Murray	Segovia
Gomez	Nancy	Seymour
Harry	Nelly	Shakespeare
Haze	Noodle	Sidney
Henry	O'Hara	Siggi
Herbert	Odd Job	Sky
Holmes	Oliver	Sophie
Homer	Oprah	Spencer
Honey	Orzo	Spike
Jack	Otis	Spirit
Jane	Pablo	Spy Master
Jazz	Peewee	Sushi
Leona	Poirot	Sylvia
Louise	Potter	Tai Pan
Loupi	Potts	Tank
Lucas	Priscilla	Tattoo
Lucy	Prozac	Theo
McDoogle	Queenie	Thor
Mabel	Ramon	Thug
Mack	Reggie	Thunder
Maggie	Rocky	Toot
Magic	Rosie	Tucker
Max	Ruby	Violet
Meanie	Sally	Walter
Molly	Samson	Wheatly
Montana	Sasha	Will
Murphy	Sebastian	Wilt

Winnefred	Yul	Zeus
Winnie	Zaki	Zoloft
X-Man	Zeke	Zorba
Yates	Zelda	Zsa Zsa